商务英语专业"互联网＋"创新型教材

2018 年第一批教育部——开元电子产学合作协同育人项目——"应用型本科院校商务英语专业创新创业一体化人才培养模式研究"成果之一（项目编号：201801222045）

2018 年教育部——北京数通国软产学合作协同育人项目——"应用型本科院校商务英语专业课程体系'需求分析'模型的构建"研究成果之一（项目编号：201801148010）

商务英语口语教程

主　编　蒋景东　　柳延东　　陈国雄
副主编　李玉娟　　董　江　　陈　珉
参　编　谭　兴　　何冬云　　汤文瑞
　　　　赖海威　　邓　萍　　孙秀娟
主　审　司汝军

机械工业出版社

本书坚持以应用为导向,以商务英语口语实践为主线编写,以模块情境教学引领、单元学习作为基本逻辑框架,将职场交际理念与语言综合训练相结合,体现了知识学习和技能训练兼顾的原则,突出了实践操作性。

本书在体例上共 4 个 Module,23 个 Unit。每个 Unit 包括三个部分:Part I Preparing, Part II Performing 和 Part III Practicing。其中,Part I Preparing 包括 Work individually 和 Pair work 两个方面的内容;Part II Performing 包括 Reading 和 Listening 两个方面的内容,Reading 分为 New Words and Phrases 和 Group work 两个方面的内容,Listening 分为 Useful Expressions 和 Pair work 两个方面的内容;Part III Practicing 包括 Reading 和 Speaking 两个部分,Reading 分为 New Words and Phrases 和 Work individually 两个方面的内容,Speaking 分为 New Words and Phrases 和 Pair work 两个方面的内容。

本书适合应用型本科院校和高职高专的学生使用,既可以作为独立的商务英语口语实训教材使用,也可作为相关专业的配套教材。

为方便教学,本书配备电子课件和听力答案等教学资源。凡选用本书作为教材的教师均可登录机械工业出版社教材服务网 www.cmpedu.com 免费下载。如有问题,请致电 010-88379375 咨询。

图书在版编目(CIP)数据

商务英语口语教程/蒋景东主编. —北京:机械工业出版社,2018.12(2024.7 重印)

商务英语专业"互联网+"创新型教材

ISBN 978-7-111-61353-4

Ⅰ.①商… Ⅱ.①蒋… Ⅲ.①商务-英语-口语-高等学校-教材 Ⅳ.①F7

中国版本图书馆 CIP 数据核字(2018)第 259798 号

机械工业出版社(北京市百万庄大街 22 号 邮政编码 100037)
策划编辑:杨晓昱 责任编辑:杨晓昱 孟晓琳
责任校对:黄兴伟 责任印制:单爱军
北京虎彩文化传播有限公司印刷

2024 年 7 月第 1 版·第 6 次印刷
184mm×260mm·12.5 印张·292 千字
标准书号:ISBN 978-7-111-61353-4
定价:39.80 元

电话服务 网络服务
客服电话:010-88361066 机 工 官 网:www.cmpbook.com
010-88379833 机 工 官 博:weibo.com/cmp1952
010-68326294 金 书 网:www.golden-book.com
封底无防伪标均为盗版 机工教育服务网:www.cmpedu.com

P*reface* 前 言

商务英语专业的培养目标是培养德、智、体、美全面发展，具有爱国主义情怀，能胜任国际贸易、市场营销、企业管理、金融、证券、物流、人力资源和旅游等行业跨文化交际活动的全面发展的实用复合型人才。该专业为大型企业培养外事招待员、商务秘书和金融服务人员；为中小型企业培养外贸业务员、辅助型行业管理员和营销员；为各种展会培养商务口译人员。其培养目标具体可分解为知识目标、能力目标和素质目标。知识目标要求学生掌握英语会话、综合英语、商务文化等语言和人文知识，熟悉国际贸易、管理学、金融学和市场营销等方面的基础商务理论；能力目标是培养学生的语言应用能力、商务实践能力和跨文化沟通交际能力；素质目标是提高学生的社会责任感、团队协作精神和道德情操，使学生成为具有良好的人文素养的职场通才。

商务英语口语是"语言知识＋商务知识＋实践交际技能＋文化背景知识"的综合性应用，需要科学性与艺术性相结合，这决定了商务英语课程的特殊性。这种特殊性大大增加了商务英语口语实训的难度。商务英语口语课程主要是培养商务环境下的口语交际技能，这种交际实践具有很强的灵活性、艺术性和权变性，如果没有大量亲身参与商务口语实践，这些技能是很难通过传统的说教方式培养的。

本书在传统商务英语口语教学的基础上，通过"互联网＋"，将互联网与商务英语教学进行深度融合，充分发挥互联网在商务英语口语教学中的优化和集成作用。

本书结合作者多年的教学经验和商务经验，以商务英语专业的培养目标为基准，借鉴国内外的先进教学方法，结合教学实际，设计了系统的口语实训体系，即以情境模块教学引领，以单元任务作为基本逻辑框架，将职场交际理念与语言综合训练相结合。本书中每个口语实训任务都采用了目前流行的、颇受学生欢迎的仿真模拟训练。

本书在体例上共 4 个 Module，23 个 Unit。每个 Unit 包括三个部分：Part I Preparing，Part II Performing 和 Part III Practicing。其中，Part I Preparing 部分包括 Work individually 和 Pair work 两个方面的内容；Part II Performing 包括 Reading 和 Listening 两个方面的内容，Reading 分为 New Words and Phrases 和 Group work 两个方面的内容，Listening 分为 Useful Expressions 和 Pair work 两个方面的内容；Part III Practicing 包括 Reading 和 Speaking 两个部分，Reading 分为 New Words and Phrases 和 Work individually 两个方面的内容，Speaking 分为 New Words and Phrases 和 Pair work 两个方面的内容。

本书具有如下特色：

1. 教学目标上的创新。注重三维目标，即知识与技能、过程与方法、情感态度与价值观，体现了显性教学和隐性教学相结合的原则。

2. 教学理念上的创新。以学生为本，凸显"导"字，通过 Part I Preparing 进行引导，进行参与式教学，教师从主讲人、管理者变为导演者、导航者，学生不再是教师灌输知识的被动接收者、被监督者，而是全面参与教学设计，自我管理的课堂主人，充分体现了"教、学、做"合一的理念。

3. 教学内容上的创新。本书内容打破了以工作过程为主线的传统教学方式，涵盖了从与客户建立关系开始一直到整个商务流程的完成，扩大了商务口语的应用领域。每个单元的内容以能力培养为主导，以职业技能需求细化分析为根据，以满足岗位技能要求为目标，融合商务师职业资格标准，构建了"教、学、做"一体化的内容体系，以寻求语言能力的培养和商务英语知识学习的最佳结合点，将语言知识、交际技能和商务知识融为一体，从而提高学生的交际能力和处理经贸实务问题的口语应用能力，适应社会对国际商务从业人员的素质要求。

4. 教学方式上的创新。（1）本书在听力部分加入了二维码，使教学更具有互动性，同时在此基础上扩展了教学范围，使商务英语口语教学更具有无边界性，这种无边界性改变了学生的学习行为，使学生的学习更具有自主性。（2）本书建立了学生全面参与的教学体系，从教学理念、教学组织形式，到多媒体教学、系列化口语实训，全过程开放，构建了由学生参与的立体化、系统化的系统，把教学的时空视野从课堂内扩大到课堂外，实现了教学渠道与空间的多元化与立体化。

本书集本科院校和国家示范性高职建设院校的教学科研之所长。参与本书编写事宜的院校有贺州学院（本科院校）、温州职业技术学院（国家示范性高职建设院校）和盐城工业职业技术学院（江苏省示范性高职建设院校）。

本书主编由贺州学院的蒋景东、柳延东和陈国雄担任；主审由北京数通国软有限公司的司汝军担任；副主编由盐城工业职业技术学院的李玉娟和温州职业技术学院的董江、陈珉担任；贺州学院的谭兴、何冬云、汤文瑞、赖海威、邓萍和孙秀娟参加编写。

本书是校企合作开发教材，是 2018 年第一批教育部开元电子产学合作协同育人项目——"应用型本科院校商务英语专业创新创业一体化人才培养模式研究"成果之一（项目编号：201801222045）；2018 年教育部——北京数通国软产学合作协同育人项目——"应用型本科院校商务英语专业课程体系'需求分析'模型的构建"研究成果之一（项目编号：201801148010）；也是贺州学院商务英语课程建设的阶段性成果之一。

本书适合应用型本科院校和高职高专的学生使用，既可以作为独立的商务英语口语实训教材使用，也可作为相关专业的配套教材使用。

本书在编写过程中，参阅了国内外许多优秀教材、专著和相关资料，引用了其中一些内容和研究成果，恕不一一详尽说明，仅在参考文献中列出，在此向有关作者致以衷心的感谢！

由于编者水平有限，书中难免有错误和不妥之处，敬请各位读者不吝赐教！

编 者

2018 年 8 月

C*ontents* 目 录

Module 1

Routine Situation

Unit 1 Office Work

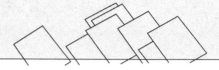

—— Objectives ——

In this unit, the students are required to grasp the following contents.

1. Learning to talk something about office work with some given useful words and phrases of this unit freely.
2. Learning to talk something about office work with some given useful sentences of this unit freely.
3. Reading a passage about office work and then paraphrasing it.
4. Listening and having a role play about office work.

······ Part I   Preparing ······

 Work individually: How often do you like to do these things in your office?

In your office, you like...	Often	Sometimes	Never
to work alone			
to work with a partner			
to work on a small group			
to work in a team			
to play computer			
to do some work in the given time			

 Pair work: Compare your answers with a partner.

I never play computer in office, especially in working hours. What about you?

······ Part II Performing ······

Reading

═══ New Words and Phrases ═══

ballpark [ˈbɔːlpɑːk] *adj.* 相近的，估算的

figure [ˈfɪɡə(r)] *n.* 人物；数字；身材；算术

profit [ˈprɒfɪt] *n.* 利润

regular [ˈreɡjələ(r)] *adj.* 有规律的；规则的，整齐的；不变的；合格的

refuse [rɪˈfjuːz] *v.* 拒绝；回绝；推却

overtime [ˈəʊvətaɪm] *n.* 加班；加班费；加时赛；超出的时间，额外的时间

in the middle of 在……中间

a ballpark figure 大概的数字

bottom line 要旨；底价

turn... into... 把……变成……

CFO＝Chief Financial Officer 首席财务官

out of the red 不再亏损

in sick 生病的

be laid off 被裁员；下岗；失业

graveyard shift 全体夜班的工人；夜班

Group work：Read the following sentences and learn how to use them freely.

1. In the middle of something? 正在忙某事吗？

2. What are you up to? 你正在做什么？

3. Can you just give me a ballpark figure? 能不能给我一个大概的数字？

4. Bottom line：we have to turn into profit by 2022.
   最重要的是：我们必须在 2002 年前转亏为盈。

5. The new CFO was sent to bring the company out of the red.
   这位新的财务长被派来把公司从赤字中拯救出来。

6. Shelly just called in sick. 雪莉刚打电话来请病假。

7. I just heard that seven people are going to be laid off next month.
   我刚听到公司下个月要裁七位员工。

8. He suggested we should go to eat after my graveyard shift.
   他建议说我们可以在我的大夜班之后一起去吃东西。

9. I am only a regular 9-to-5er. 我只是一个平凡的朝九晚五上班族。

10. I refuse to work overtime during the weekend. 我拒绝在周末时加班。

11. I'll put her on the phone. Just a second. 我将请她听电话，请等一下。

12. I'm transferring your call. / I'm redirecting your call. 我帮你转接（分机）。

13. Would you mind holding for one minute? 你是否介意等一分钟?

14. He's out for lunch. Would you like to try again an hour later?
    他出去吃午餐了。你要不要一小时后再打来?

15. She is not here but you can call her telephone answering machine.
    她不在这里，但是你可以打她的电话答录机。

Listening 🎧

════════ Useful Expressions ════════

General Manager 总经理   at the moment 此刻

call sb. back 给某人回电话   be convenient for 对……方便

give sth. to sb. 把某物给某人   come back 回来

Pair work: Listen to the dialogues and fill in the blanks.

════ Dialogue 1 ════

Office Telephone（1）

音频 1-1

A: General Manager's Office. _____?

B: Yes，_____ Mr. Muller，please?

A: I'm sorry. He's in a meeting at the moment. _____?

B: Yes，please. When he _____, please tell him that David Charles called. Could he call me back before _____? It's _____.

A: Of course. Does he know your _____?

B: I think he does. But you _____ give it to him again. That's 82375598.

A: Can I check that? It's 82375598.

B: That's right.

A: OK，I'll _____ Mr. Muller _____ he comes back.

B: Thank you very much. Goodbye.

A: Goodbye.

════ Dialogue 2 ════

Office Telephone（2）

音频 1-2

A: Good afternoon，Miss Lily. This is John from Shanghai ABM Company. I'm calling to _____ you for sometime tomorrow.

B: Hello，Mr. John. I'll _____. I'm sorry I'm quite busy on Wednesday. In the morning, I'm _____. In the afternoon，I'm seeing someone from the _____. How about Thursday?

A: _____. Would 10:30 a. m. be convenient for you?

B: Let me see. Sorry，I'm afraid I can't _____ in the morning because I'm having _____.

A: Then can you _____ in the afternoon?

B: Yes. Would 4:00 p. m. be all right?

A: Yes，_____.

B: Then I'll see you on Thursday afternoon at 4:00.

A: I _____，Miss Lily. Goodbye.

B: Bye.

﹒﹒﹒﹒﹒﹒ Part III Practicing ﹒﹒﹒﹒﹒﹒

Reading

==== New Words and Phrases ====

professional [prəˈfeʃənl] *adj.* 专业的；职业的；专业性的

administrative [ədˈmɪnɪstrətɪv] *adj.* 管理的，行政的

include [ɪnˈkluːd] *v.* 包括

equipment [ɪˈkwɪpmənt] *n.* 设备

environment [ɪnˈvaɪrənmənt] *n.* 环境

productively [prəˈdʌktɪvli] *adv.* 有结果地，有成果地

ergonomics [ˌɜːɡəˈnɒmɪks] *n.* 工效学；人类工程学

temperature [ˈtemprətʃə(r)] *n.* 温度

ventilation [ˌventɪˈleɪʃn] *n.* 通风设备；空气流通；通风方法

decoration [ˌdekəˈreɪʃn] *n.* 装饰

depend on 依赖，依靠

be involved in 卷入，涉及，参与

apply to 适合，适用于……，向……提出申请

lay out 展示；设计；安排；陈设

in relation to 与……有关

be suitable for 适于；合适

emphasis on 强调

🦢 Work individually：Read the following passage and then paraphrase.

What is Office Work?

An office is a room where professional duties and administrative work is carried out. The details of the work depend on the type of business that you are involved in, but usually in-

5

clude using computers, communicating with others by telephone or fax, keeping records and files etc. Features of an office such as people, space, equipment, furniture and the environment, must fit together well for workers to feel healthy and comfortable and to be able to work efficiently and productively. This is what ergonomics can help!

Ergonomics can be applied to offices in several ways. You could look at how the office is laid out, including where people sit in relation to equipment, windows, doors and each other. You could check that equipment and furniture is suitable for the type of work that people are doing. This includes seats, desks, computers, printers and anything else that they might use to do their job. You could assess the environment that is, the temperature, ventilation, lighting, decoration. All these aspects of an office are considered in relation to the individuals in the office with emphasis on their safety, health, comfort and productivity!

Speaking

New Words and Phrases

schedule ['skedʒuːl] *n.* 时刻表 *v.* 排定，安排；将……列表；为……做目录

contract ['kɒntrækt] *n.* 合同

company ['kʌmpəni] *n.* 公司

processing ['prəʊsesɪŋ] *n.* 处理，工序，过程

manufacturing [ˌmænjuˈfæktʃərɪŋ] *adj.* 生产的

efficiently [ɪˈfɪʃntli] *adv.* 有效率地

redesign [ˌriːdɪˈzaɪn] *v.* 重新设计

furniture ['fɜːnɪtʃə(r)] *n.* 家私，家具

atmosphere ['ætməsfɪə(r)] *n.* 气氛

simultaneously [ˌsɪmlˈteɪnɪəsli] *adv.* 同时地，同一时间地

well-equipped 设备齐全的

install computer 安装电脑

management code 管理规范

office automation 办公室自动化

equip... with 用……装备……

network of workstations 工作站网络

as soon as possible（简称 ASAP）尽快

limited in function 有限的功能

sign the contract with 与……签合同

What about...? ……怎么样？

production manager 生产经理，生产部经理

department meeting 部门会议

office equipment 办公设备

 Pair work: Listen to the dialogues and have a role play.

音频 1-3

Dialogue 1

With a New Employee

A: Hi there! My name's Terry Graham. You're new around here?

B: Yes. My name's Mark Benson. I just started a couple of weeks ago.

A: Well, if there's anything I can do for you, let me know.

B: Thanks, I appreciate that!

音频 1－4

 Dialogue 2

With the General Manager

A: Hello, Ms. Barkley. How are you?

B: Fine, thank you, sir. It's nice to see you again.

A: Good to see you again, too. How's you family?

B: Very well, thank you, Mr. Parker.

音频 1－5

Dialogue 3

Checking Schedule

M: Hello, Cathy. It's Tom. Could you check my schedule for the next week?

W: Well, on Monday you are to sign the contract with Auden Company at 9:30.

M: Fine. What about Tuesday?

W: On Tuesday you're going to attend the sales meeting at 10:00. And you're in France from Wednesday afternoon through to the weekend.

M: So I'm free on Tuesday afternoon and Wednesday morning. Right?

W: Not on Wednesday morning. You'll meet the new production manager at 9:00. But you'll be free on Tuesday afternoon.

M: Thanks, Cathy. I'll see if I can schedule the department meeting for then. Could you enter it in my schedule first?

W: Yes, I'll do that.

M: Have a good weekend! Bye.

W: Bye, Mr. Barnes.

音频 1－6

Dialogue 4

Modernizing Computer

John: If we are to modernize our information processing, manufacturing system and management code, we need to complete our office automation.

Mary: Yes, you're right. We have to equip our company with a network of workstations at every office as soon as possible.

John: Our copying machines are too slow, our telephone system is limited in function, and our offices are not well-equipped for us to work efficiently. To improve the offices for higher efficiency, we also have to change all the chairs and some of the desks, redesign our office so that we may have more space.

Mary: Good. We can contact the Tianfa Office Furniture Store, and ask them to install computers in our company, deliver new tables and other furniture to match the function of the computers, and to improve our work atmosphere simultaneously.

Unit 2 Communication

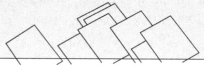

━━━━━ Objectives ━━━━━

In this unit, the students are required to grasp the following contents.

1. Learning to talk something about communication with some given useful words and phrases of this unit freely.
2. Learning to talk something about communication with some given useful sentences of this unit freely.
3. Reading a passage about communication and then paraphrasing it.
4. Listening and having a role play about communication.

······ Part I Preparing ······

 Work individually: How often do you like to do when you communicate with others?

In your communication, you like...	Often	Sometimes	Never
to talk about customs			
to talk about driving and cars			
to talk about entrepreneurs			
to talk about family values			
to talk about success and failure			
to talk about environmental problems			

 Pair work: Compare your answers with a partner.

I do not like to communicate with others in office, especially in working hours. What about you?

······ Part II Performing ······

Reading

New Words and Phrases

extension [ɪk'stenʃn] *n.* 电话分机

dial ['daɪəl] *v.* 拨（电话号码）

operator ['ɒpəreɪtə(r)] *n.* 接线员

podcast ['pɒdkɑːst] *n.* 博客

available [ə'veɪləbl] *adj.* 有空的

emergency [ɪ'mɜːdʒənsi] *n.* 紧急情况

memo ['meməʊ] *n.* 备忘录

applicability [ˌæplɪk'bɪləti] *n.* 适用性

stipulate ['stɪpjuleɪt] *v.* 规定，保证

jargon ['dʒɑːgən] *n.* 行话，术语

acronym ['ækrənɪm] *n.* 首字母缩略词

snobbery ['snɒbəri] *n.* 势力

iPod 苹果音乐播放器

cutting-edge 前沿的

working/office hours 办公时间

area code 区号

communications expert 通信专家

news feeds 新闻推送

Group work：Read the following sentences and learn how to use them freely.

1. making a phone call 打电话

2. answering a phone call 接电话

3. forms of communication 沟通模式

4. nonverbal communication 非口头信息交流

5. selecting language appropriate to the audience 选择适合听众的语言

6. receiving criticism without defensiveness 接受批评

7. showing an interest in others，asking about and recognizing their feelings
   表现出对他人的兴趣，询问并认识他们的感受

8. speaking confidently but with modesty 自信而谦逊地说话

9. summarizing key points made by other speakers 总结其他发言者的要点

10. supporting statements with facts and evidence 用事实和证据支持陈述的内容

11. conveying messages concisely 简明传达信息

12. paraphrasing to show understanding 解读以示理解

13. speaking calmly even when you're stressed 即使你有压力，也要心平气和地说话

14. speaking at a moderate pace，not too fast or too slowly
    以中等速度说话，不要太快或太慢

15. stating your needs，wants or feelings without criticizing or blaming
    不要用批评或责备的口气来陈述你的需求、欲望或者感受

Listening

═══ **Useful Expressions** ═══

How are you doing recently? 你最近过得怎么样？

communicate with 与……联系，与……交往；与……相通

contact with 与……有交往［联系］　　　ways of communication 通信方式；交流方式

mobile phone 移动电话　　　　　　　at any time 随时；任何时候

be suitable for 适于；合适　　　　　go over 重温；翻；转为；留下印象；搁置起来

in the summary documents 在总结文件中

Pair work：Listen to the dialogues and fill in the blanks.

音频 2-1

═══ Dialogue 1 ═══

Communication（1）

S: Hi，Mark，I haven't seen you for ＿＿＿＿＿＿.

M: Hi，Sunny. It's nice to see you again! How are you doing ＿＿＿＿＿＿?

S: Not bad. ＿＿＿＿＿ you?

M: Well，＿＿＿＿＿＿.

S: How do you think，a long time ago，people ＿＿＿＿＿＿＿＿ others?

M: Well，I know，they usually write，＿＿＿＿＿＿＿. You know，it's not ＿＿＿＿＿ ＿＿＿＿＿ much time. But some people still ＿＿＿＿＿ other through letters，they think writing can bring ＿＿＿＿＿＿＿＿＿.

S: Yes，but with the progress of the ＿＿＿＿＿，there are many ways to ＿＿＿＿＿，such as mobile phone，E-mail，QQ and so on. I believe different people have different choices for the ＿＿＿＿＿＿＿. And what do you ＿＿＿＿＿＿?

M: Uh... I like to use ＿＿＿＿＿＿，and I always take it ＿＿＿＿＿＿＿. I think it's much more ＿＿＿＿＿ me. How about you?

S: Oh，I usually use QQ to communicate，because QQ has become very ＿＿＿＿＿ for its convenience.

M: Oh，it's ＿＿＿＿＿ class. See you later.

S: See you.

===== Dialogue 2 =====

Communication（2）

音频 2-2

Chairman: I'd like to open today's meeting. Does everyone _____ of the agenda? Mary, you first.

Mary: Thank you，Sir. I'll quickly _____ the main points of our _____. I suggest each one of us give _____ on the research we've done on the suggestions discussed last week.

Chairman: You'll find most of the _____ in the summary documents in front of you.

Mary: These figures are interesting. It's clear to me that customer _____ are not as _____ as they could be.

Chairman: It's true. Our _____ really haven't been effective to date.

Mary: I suggest we _____ into groups and discuss how we can _____ _____ our message.

Chairman: That's a good idea. Let's do that and meet _____ again in 20 minutes so that we can continue and complete today's _____.

······ Part III Practicing ······

Reading

===== New Words and Phrases =====

exchange [ɪks'tʃeɪndʒ] *n. v.* 交换

accountability [ə'kaʊntə'bɪləti] *n.* 责任制；有责任，有义务

harmonize ['hɑːmənaɪz] *v.* 使和谐；和谐

chemistry ['kemɪstri] *n.* 化学

hidden ['hɪdn] *adj.* 隐藏的；神秘的

agenda [ə'dʒendə] *n.* 议事日程

impact ['ɪmpækt] *n.* 影响；冲击

exchange of messages 交换信息

hidden agenda 另有企图

Work individually： Read the following passage and then paraphrase.

===== Communication =====

What's Communication?

Communication is the exchange of messages between people for the purpose of achieving common meaning. Or it can be defined as the process by which information is exchanged and understood by two or more people.

Importance of Communication

- We must communicate
- You're communicating anywhere and anytime
- You must afford the results and accountability
- Related to your harmonize personal relationship
- Make you more influence
- Impact your future development

Why cannot communicate?

- Words difference
- Unequal information：Fact vs Viewpoint
- Different people：Sense of word/Former experience/Incompatibility（个性不合）
- Different speed
- Different status in organization
- Time difference
- Hidden agenda

Speaking

New Words and Phrases

describe [dɪˈskraɪb] *v.* 叙述；描写

frame [freɪm] *v.* 设计

gorgeous [ˈgɔːdʒəs] *adj.* 华丽的，艳丽的

decorate [ˈdekəreɪt] *v.* 装饰；点缀

personality [ˌpɜːsəˈnæləti] *n.* 生而为人；人格，人品，个性；人物

promote [prəˈməʊt] *v.* 促进，推进；提升

insight [ˈɪnsaɪt] *n.* 顿悟；领悟；洞察力

photo frame 照相架

wedding day 婚礼，结婚纪念日；婚期；佳期

wedding photographs 结婚照

nothing but 无非；只有，只不过

a sales meeting 销售会议

 Pair work：Listen to the dialogues and have a role play.

Dialogue 1

Selling a Product

John: So，Lesley. Show us how you would describe your product.

Lesley: My product is called "Mr & Mrs photo frame". Your wedding day is one of the most important days of your life，and it's a day you'll remember forever! Make sure you

音频 2-3

frame your wedding photographs in nothing but the best. Look no further than our gorgeous "Mr & Mrs photo frame"!

John: Hmmm. Nice!

Lesley: Its design is modern. This is a frame that will stand out! It is made only from the highest quality materials, and it is beautifully decorated.

John: Okay, not bad.

Lesley: Bring a touch of personality to your home or office, or send a gift in your friend's way! Order now!

John: I like your product a lot. And I like the way you promoted it.

Lesley: Thank you, Sir.

━━━━ Dialogue 2 ━━━━

A Sales Meeting

音频 2 - 4

Alice: We're having a sales meeting tomorrow. Can you make it?

Kevin: At what time?

Alice: It should be at 10 o'clock. Is that OK?

Kevin: Yes, that'll be fine.

Alice: We're going to go over some suggestions to improve communication with customers.

Kevin: Good. I have some suggestions I'd like to make.

Alice: Frank is also going to make some suggestions on improving sales in China.

Kevin: That'll be interesting. He's got keen insights.

Alice: Yes, he's going to outline some new sales strategies.

Kevin: Is Alan attending?

Alice: No, he's flying to San Francisco and won't be able to make it.

Unit 3 Paid Vacation

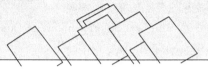

═══ Objectives ═══

In this unit, the students are required to grasp the following contents.

1. Learning to talk something about paid vacation with some given useful words and phrases of this unit freely.
2. Learning to talk something about paid vacation with some given useful sentences of this unit freely.
3. Reading a passage about paid vacation and then paraphrasing it.
4. Listening and having a role play about paid vacation.

······ Part I   Preparing ······

 Work individually: How often do you like to do these things in your vacation?

In your vacation, you like...	Often	Sometimes	Never
to travel alone			
to travel with friends			
to go to the mountains			
to visit some places of interests			
to go to the beach			
to do some work in the given time			

 Pair work: Compare your answers with a partner.

I like travelling during my paid vacation. What about you?

······ Part II　Performing ······

Reading

New Words and Phrases

dividend ['dɪvɪdend] *n.* 红利，股息，股利

bonus ['bəʊnəs] *n.* 奖金，津贴；额外的好处，意外收获

canteen [kæn'tiːn] *n.*（工厂、商店、高校的）食堂，餐厅

company benefits 公司福利

career planning 职业规划

preference shares 优先股

day care（针对儿童、老人、病人等的）日托，日间看护

flexible hours 灵活的工作时间

paid holiday 带薪休假

gym membership 健身房会员资格

company car 公司配车

mobile phone 手机

annual bonus /year-end bonus 年度奖

 Group work：Read the following sentences and learn how to use them freely.

1. go on vacation 去度假

   go on a vacation 侧重于某一次具体的度假

2. go on a beach vacation 进行一次沙滩度假

3. go on a nice vacation 进行一次愉快的度假/旅行

4. You can have Saturdays and Sundays off. 你可以在周六和周日不工作。

5. Besides you may have a paid month holiday every year.

   此外，你每年可休一个月的带薪假。

6. We would like to start you off at 1,500 *yuan* a month, not including bonus and overtime pay. 我们可以付你起薪每月 1,500 元，不包括奖金和加班费。

7. We don't give bonus every month，but we offer a semiannual bonuses.

   并非每月都有奖金，但我们每半年发奖金。

8. And you will receive two weeks' paid vacation a year，as well.

   此外你还可以有每年两周的带薪假期。

9. Does it suit you? 你觉得合适吗？

10. Our girls have a three-week vacation a year.

    我们的女职工每年有三个星期的假期。

11. We'll supply you with an apartment of two bedrooms and a living room.

    我们会给你一套两室一厅的公寓房。

12. Are you familiar with our pay scale? 你熟悉我们的工资级别吗？

13. We offer 1% commission on all your sales.

    对你的销售额，我们将给予 1% 的佣金。

14. You'll also enjoy life insurance and health insurance，a two-week paid vacation a year，a five-day work week.

你将享受人寿保险和健康保险，一年一次为期两周的带薪假，每周工作五天。

15. You'll get bonus at the end of each year. 年底你会得到年终奖金。

Listening 🎧

═══════ **Useful Expressions** ═══════

vacation [vəˈkeɪʃn] *n.* 假期，休假　　　　waterfall [ˈwɔːtəfɔːl] *n.* 瀑布

take some time off 抽出一些时间　　　　annual vacation 年假

long time no see 好久不见

Pair work：Listen to the dialogues and fill in the blanks.

═══════ Dialogue 1 ═══════

音频 3-1

About Vacation（1）

A: I've been working hard for _____. I really need a _____.

B: That's true. You need to take some time off to _____.

A: You said it. I'm looking forward to my _____.

B: When are you going to _____?

A: Later this month. I can't wait!

B: I really _____ you. I'm not _____ until December.

═══════ Dialogue 2 ═══════

音频 3-2

About Vacation（2）

Rick：Hi，Helen. Long time no see.

Helen：Hi，Rick. Yes，I was on vacation last month.

Rick：Oh，did you go anywhere _____?

Helen：Yes，I went to Guizhou with my _____.

Rick：Wow! Did you see Huangguoshu _____?

Helen：Yes，I did. It was _____! We took _____ photos there. What about you? Did you do _____ last month?

Rick：Not really. I just stayed at home most of the time to _____ and _____.

······· Part III　Practicing ·······

Reading

======= New Words and Phrases =======

employee [ɪmˈplɔiː] *n.* 雇工，雇员

voluntary [ˈvɒləntri] *n.* 自愿者 *adj.* 志愿的；自愿的

generous [ˈdʒenərəs] *adj.* 慷慨的，大方的；丰盛的

accrue [əˈkruː] *v.* 增加；获得

accrual [əˈkruːəl] *n.* 利息；获利

forfeit [ˈfɔːfɪt] *v.* 丧失，失去

state-mandated 国家规定的

European Union 欧洲联盟

mandated amount 规定的金额

accrue time 累积时间

access to 有权使用

 Work individually: Read the following passage and then paraphrase.

What is Paid Vacation?

Paid vacation is a benefit offered to employees that may be voluntary on the part of the company or state-mandated. The most generous paid time packages exist in the European Union. Especially where employees do not have mandated amount of paid time, amount of time given may depend on a variety of factors — not least among these is the company's rules regarding paid vacation.

Where paid vacation exists, workers may accrue time on a weekly basis adding a certain amount of hours per week to their vacation total. Other companies give employees access to all their year's vacation time at the beginning of employment. The accrual method is more common, however. If employees are laid off during a work year, the company might have to pay them the amount of vacation time accrued, although this is not always the case. Moreover some vacation time is offered on a "use it or lose it" basis and employees may have to take the time within a certain established period or forfeit it.

Speaking

======= New Words and Phrases =======

obstacle [ˈɒbstəkl] *n.* 障碍物；障碍

encounter [ɪnˈkaʊntə(r)] *v.* 遭遇；不期而遇

remarkable [rɪˈmɑːkəbl] *adj.* 显著的；卓越的

goof off 混日子，逃避工作

stumbling block 障碍，绊脚石

bottom line 要旨，起码的要求

maternity leave 产假

endowment insurance 养老保险

medical insurance 医疗保险

unemployment insurance 失业保险

employment injury insurance 工伤保险

maternity insurance 生育保险

Housing Provident Fund 住房公积金

paid vacation 带薪休假

paid annual vacation 带薪年度休假

vacation jobs 假期工作

volunteer vacation /volunteer holiday 义工度假

minor vacation 小长假

 Pair work： Listen to the dialogues and have a role play.

━━━ **Dialogue 1** ━━━

音频 3 - 3

Where did you go on vacation？（1）

M： Grace，where did you go on vacation?

W： I went to New York City.

M： Oh，really? Did you go with anyone?

W： Yes，I went with my mother. Where did you go on vacation?

M： I went to Huangshan.

W： Oh，really? Did you go with anyone?

M： Yes，I went with my friends. We were very happy.

━━━ **Dialogue 2** ━━━

音频 3 - 4

Where did you go on vacation？（2）

Girl： What did you do on vacation，Sally?

Sally： Nothing. I just stayed at home.

Girl： And did you do anything interesting，Bob?

Bob： Yes，I visited my uncle. We went fishing，but we didn't get any fish. Did you go anywhere on vacation，Girl?

Girl： I went to summer camp.

Sally： Did you go with anyone，Girl?

Girl： Yes，I went with my friends. Everyone had a great time.

Xiang Hua： Hey，Tina. Where did you go on vacation?

Tina： I went to the mountains with my family.

Xiang Hua： Did everyone have a good time?

Tina： Oh，yes. Everything was excellent. Where did you go，Xiang Hua?

Xiang Hua： I went to New York City.

Unit 4 Business Ethics

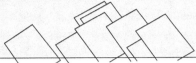

In this unit, the students are required to grasp the following contents.

1. Learning to talk something about business ethics with some given useful words and phrases of this unit freely.

2. Learning to talk something about business ethics with some given useful sentences of this unit freely.

3. Reading a passage about business ethics and then paraphrasing it.

4. Listening and having a role play about business ethics.

.... Part I Preparing ....

 Work individually: How often do you like to do these things about business ethics?

About business ethics you like...	Often	Sometimes	Never
keeping secret			
researching business secret protection system			
refusing to accept kickbacks			
refusing to accept bribery			
following the applicable business ethics			
knowing right from wrong			

 Pair work: Compare your answers with a partner.

I never violate business ethics. What about you?

······ **Part II Performing** ······

Reading

═══ New Words and Phrases ═══

incompleteness ['ɪnkəm'pliːtnəs] *n.* 不完全

espionage ['espɪɒnɑːʒ] *n.* 间谍活动；侦察

bribery ['braɪbəri] *n.* 行贿；[法] 贿赂

kickback ['kɪkbæk] *n.* 佣金，回扣

outsourcing ['aʊtsɔːsɪŋ] *n.* 外购；外部采办

disclose [dɪs'kləʊz] *vt.* 公开；揭露

imbalance [ɪm'bæləns] *n.* 不平衡；失调

moderate ['mɒdərət] *adj.* 有节制的；稳健的，温和的

legislation [ˌledʒɪs'leɪʃn] *n.* 立法，制定法律；法律，法规

strife [straɪf] *n.* 冲突；斗争

malice ['mælɪs] *n.* 怨恨；恶意

disruptive [dɪs'rʌptɪv] *adj.* 破坏的；分裂性的；扰乱的

computer equipment 计算机设备

secret business 内幕交易

the definition of the right 权利界定

top-secret work 绝密工作

a self-disciplining system 自律机制

the system of "China Wall" "中国墙" 制度

worth referential to 值得……借鉴

intelligent property right 知识产权

a knowledge property 知识财产

job-hopping 跳槽

business secret 商业秘密

business strife 竞业

reasonable restriction 合理的限制

tailor-made service 个性化服务

fast-paced 快速地

co-development 共发展

business secret protection law 商业秘密保护法

the world legislation for business secret protection

世界商业秘密保护立法；世界商业秘密立法

Group work：Read the following expressions and sentences and learn how to use them freely.

1. the legislation of business secret protection 商业秘密保护立法

2. the focus of the Business Secret Protection Law 商业秘密保护法的重心

3. adopt reasonable restriction to prohibit business strife in legislation
   在立法上采取合理的限制以禁止竞业

4. a hot issue in the legislation circle across the world 世界各国立法的热点问题

5. professional and tailor-made service; extraordinary quality
   专业和个性化的服务；意料之外的质量

6. an undisputable fact 一个不争的事实

7. keep the reputation of the company 维护公司名誉

8. disruptive of business practices 商业经营的破坏

9. Every business has valuable proprietary data. 每家企业都有有价值的专有数据。

10. lack of adherence to standard business ethics 缺乏对公共商业道德规范的遵守

11. I'm only thinking of the company's best interests. 我只是为公司的最大利益着想。

12. People make decisions within organizations every day. 人们每天都在组织里做决策。

13. For the most part，they do so with the interests of the organization in mind.
他们这样做多半都是在为组织的利益着想。

14. The challenge for organizations is to ensure that decisions are not only profitable，but that they are ethical as well. 一个组织做出的决策不光要有利可图，还要符合基本的道德规范，这也是组织所面临的挑战。

15. Anything beyond a preset monetary value must be declared or turned in to the company.
任何超出预先规定价值标准的物品都必须向公司声明或上交。

Listening

━━━━━ **Useful Expressions** ━━━━━

acknowledged [əkˈnɒlɪdʒd] *adj.* 公认的

specific [spɪˈsɪfɪk] *adj.* 具体的；明确的

concept [ˈkɒnsept] *n.* 观念，概念

contradiction [ˌkɒntrəˈdɪkʃn] *n.* 矛盾；否认

uphold [ʌpˈhəʊld] *v.* 支持；维持

standard [ˈstændəd] *n.* 标准，规格

integrity [ɪnˈtegrəti] *n.* 完整；正直，诚实

fraud [frɔːd] *n.* 欺诈；骗子；伪劣品；冒牌货

client [ˈklaɪənt] *n.* 顾客；当事人

clash [klæʃ] *v.* 冲突

conduct [kənˈdʌkt] *v.* 传导；引导；从事

stockholder [ˈstɒkhəʊldə(r)] *n.* 股东；股票持有者

creditor [ˈkredɪtə(r)] *n.* 债权人，债主

essential [ɪˈsenʃl] *adj.* 必要的；本质的

constantly [ˈkɒnstəntli] *adv.* 时刻；不断地

reputation [ˌrepjuˈteɪʃn] *n.* 名气，名声

tax-avoidance cheating 避税作弊

moral concern 道德关注

violate laws 违反法律

refer to 参考；指的是；涉及

in other words 换句话说；就是说

as a result 结果，因此

keep... in mind 记住……

be responsible for 为……负责，形成……的原因

Pair work：Listen to the dialogues and fill in the blanks.

━━━━━ Dialogue 1 ━━━━━

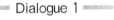

音频 4–1

Business Ethics

A: Business ethics refers to acknowledged _____ applied in specific business situations and activities. To some people，the _____ of business ethics may be a __ _____ .

B: In other words, they may view business managers as _____ only for making profits, not for upholding standards of _____.

S: While maybe that's why there are so many unethical behaviors in business activities such as _____, _____ and _____. These things erode the principle of integrity that lies at the _____ of our business organizations.

A: Maybe you are right. But I don't think business and ethics clash. Indeed, good ethics means good management.

B: If companies ignore moral concerns, _____ laws, or act unethically, they cannot possibly _____, let alone making any _____.

S: I can't agree _____. Integrity is very important in business _____ _____. Companies should apply the highest standards of integrity to everything they do. You see, without _____, a company cannot possibly gain the _____ _____ of customers, clients and the public; as a result, it will certainly fail to survive in this highly _____ age.

A: Yes, I agree with you. Companies should _____ moral principles when they _____ _____ business, because their decisions can _____ society, and they have responsibility to their _____, _____, _____ and _____ _____, etc.

B: So operating in an ethical manner is _____ to company success.

━━━━━ Dialogue 2 ━━━━━

Necessary Statement of Business Ethics

音频 4-2

S: Why do you think it is _____ for every company to have clearly stated business ethics?

A: It's essential that every company should establish _____ of business ethics and responsibilities that _____ for business activities.

B: All employees must _____ and constantly apply it to the _____ _____ of all activities for the company.

S: Besides that integrity will also create wealth. If you act with integrity _____ _____, you can enjoy _____ and a good public image. That would keep good people in your employ, and keep customers _____ your products or services.

A: That's right. I _____ you.

B: I agree with you, too.

······ Part III   Practicing ······

Reading

═══════════ New Words and Phrases ═══════════

diverse [daɪˈvɜːs] *adj.* 不同的，多种多样的

capitalism [ˈkæpɪtəlɪzəm] *n.* 资本主义（制度）；资本

association [əˌsəʊʃiˈeɪʃn] *n.* 联想；协会，社团

responsibility [rɪˌspɒnsəˈbɪləti] *n.* 责任；职责

link [lɪŋk] *n.* 环，节

adheres to 遵循，依附；附着

at large 一般说来；详细地

one-on-one 面对面的；一对一的；仅限两人之间的

bring up 提出；养育

in the chain of 在……链条中

Work individually：Read the following passage and then paraphrase.

What is Business Ethics?

Business ethics is the behavior that a business adheres to in its daily dealings with the world. The ethics of a particular business can be diverse. They apply not only to how the business interacts with the world at large，but also to their one-on-one dealings with a single customer.

Many businesses have gained a bad reputation just by being in business. To some people，businesses are interested in making money，and that is the bottom line. It could be called capitalism in its purest form. Making money is not wrong in itself. It is the manner in which some businesses conduct themselves that brings up the question of ethical behavior.

Good business ethics should be a part of every business. There are many factors to consider. When a company does business with another that is considered unethical，does this make the first company unethical by association? Some people would say yes，the first business has a responsibility and it is now a link in the chain of unethical businesses.

Many global businesses，including most of the major brands that the public use，can be seen not to think too highly of good business ethics. Many major brands have been fined millions for breaking ethical business laws. Money is the major deciding factor.

Speaking

═══════════ New Words and Phrases ═══════════

discrimination [dɪˌskrɪmɪˈneɪʃn] *n.* 歧视；辨别

harassment [ˈhærəsmənt] *n.* 袭扰；骚扰，扰乱

originate [əˈrɪdʒɪneɪt] *v.* 发源

contemporary [kənˈtemprəri] *adj.* 当代的，现代的；同时代的

normative ['nɔ:mətɪv] *adj.* 标准的，规范的

descriptive [dɪ'skrɪptɪv] *adj.* 描写的，描述的

dimension [daɪ'menʃn] *n.* 尺寸；维度

primarily [praɪ'merəli] *adv.* 首先；首要地，主要地

merriment ['merɪmənt] *n.* 欢乐，嬉戏，欢笑

diversion [daɪ'vɜːʃn] *n.* 消遣；转移；分散注意力

conspiracy [kən'spɪrəsi] *n.* 阴谋；共谋；反叛

contrivance [kən'traɪvəns] *n.* 计谋

get one's work done 完成某人的工作

Want Ads 招聘广告

have nothing to do with 与……无关

get on one's back 找……的碴儿

sexual harassment 性骚扰

personal phone calls 私人电话

be relevant to 与……有关

legal system 法制；法律体系

Pair work：Listen to the dialogues and have a role play.

Dialogue 1

音频 4-3

Lack of Adherence to Business Ethics

Shelley: Eric，why don't you do some work for a change?

Eric: What do you mean? I get my work done.

Shelley: True，but it doesn't look like you're working too hard right now.

Eric: I'm reading the newspaper to stay tuned to the business world.

Shelley: That's not very truthful，Eric. I've noticed you spend more time scanning the Want Ads than anything else.

Eric: You know，Shelley，sometimes I think you don't like me. Is it because I'm from the south?

Shelley: This has nothing to do with discrimination，Eric! I'm talking about your lack of ethics.

Eric: You're always getting on my back，Shelley. I could almost make a case for sexual harassment.

Shelley: Don't be so thick-headed，Eric. I'm not being personal，here. I'm only thinking of the company's best interests. You spend too much time on personal phone calls，surfing the net on sites that have nothing to do with our company's business，and doing personal emails. Why can't you be more honest and admit that I'm right?

Eric: I guess I do spend too much time on non-business affairs. I really admire your integrity，Shelley. I think I'll go see the boss and see if he has anything else for me to do. See you later!

━━ Dialogue 2 ━━

Connotation of Business Ethics

音频 4 - 4

A: What does business ethics apply to?

B: It applies to all aspects of business conduct and is relevant to the conduct of individuals and entire organizations.

A: That is to say, these ethics originate from individuals, organizational statements or from the legal system.

B: So business ethics refers to contemporary organizational standards, principles, sets of values and norms that govern the actions and behaviors of an individual in the business organization.

A: Business ethics has normative and descriptive dimensions. As a corporate practice and a career specialization, the field is primarily normative.

B: Adam Smith said, "People of the same trade seldom meet together, even for merriment and diversion, but the conversation ends in a conspiracy against the public, or in some contrivance to raise prices."

A: In another way saying, business ethics is a form of applied ethics or professional ethics that examines ethical principles and moral or ethical problems that arise in a business environment.

B: OK, I understand it further.

Unit 5 Products Introduction and Promotion

Objectives

In this unit, the students are required to grasp the following contents.

1. Learning to talk something about products introduction and promotion with some given useful words and phrases of this unit freely.

2. Learning to talk something about products introduction and promotion with some given useful sentences of this unit freely.

3. Reading a passage about products introduction and promotion and then paraphrasing it.

4. Listening and having a role play about products introduction and promotion.

······· Part I   Preparing ·······

Work individually: How often do you like to do these things about products introduction and promotion?

About your product introduction and promotion, you like...	Often	Sometimes	Never
to work alone			
to work with a partner			
to work on a small group			
to work in a team			
to make some advertisements			
to do some work in the given time			

Pair work: Compare your answers with a partner.

I never do anything about product introduction and promotion. What about you?

······ Part II　Performing ······

Reading

New Words and Phrases

campaign [kæm'peɪn] *n.* 活动；运动；战役

entice [ɪn'taɪs] *n.* 劝诱；怂恿

thorough ['θʌrə] *adj.* 彻底的，全面的，充分的

comprehensive [ˌkɒmprɪ'hensɪv] *adj.* 综合的；广泛的；有理解力的

substance ['sʌbstəns] *n.* 实质

testimonial [ˌtestɪ'məʊnɪəl] *n.* 推荐书；证明书

endorse [ɪn'dɔːs] *v.* 认可；支持

pitch [pɪtʃ] *n.* 推销

definitely ['defɪnətli] *adv.* 明显地；确切地

advertising campaign 广告宣传活动

make a purchase 购买

illegal representations 非法宣传

shopping mall 购物中心

door-to-door sales 挨户销售

go all out on 在……上全力以赴

Group work：Read the following sentences and learn how to use them freely.

1. What's the most famous advertising campaign you can think of?
   你所能想到的最有名的广告宣传活动是什么？

2. Advertising is the means or channel of how you make the market aware of what product/service you're selling and how to entice them to actually make a purchase.
   广告是使市场了解你所推销的产品/服务，并劝诱人们购买的一种手段或渠道。

3. To be effective, advertisement must be targeted at the right people and it must deliver the right message. 为了起到一定效果，广告必须定位准确，而且必须传达正确的信息。

4. Western business proposals are very thorough，comprehensive, detailed and purpose-oriented. 西方商业建议具有全面、综合、详尽和目标明确的特点。

5. In Western countries，almost everything goes in terms of content，style and substance.
   西方国家，几乎任何事情都分为内容、风格和实质三个方面。

6. Illegal representations or violations of the law are not condoned.
   非法的宣传或违反法规的活动是不可以赦免的。

7. Let's go all out on this one. I want a national advertising campaign.
   让我们全力以赴实施这个方案吧。我想开展一次全国范围的广告宣传活动。

8. Put a full-page ad in the newspaper every Friday，advertising the weekly special coming up. 每周五在报纸上做整版广告，为每周特卖做宣传。

9. Let's get 20,000 flyers printed. We'll hand them out at the shopping mall next weekend.

27

我们印制 20,000 份广告吧，我们要于下周末在购物中心免费派送。

10. I want this advertisement to be a testimonial from the gold medal winner. Call her to see if we can get her to endorse our product.

我希望这个广告作为来自金牌得主的推荐，给她打电话问她能不能帮忙宣传我们的产品。

11. We need a new slogan. The old one's not catchy enough.

我们需要新的口号，旧的不够吸引人。

12. If we want to try door-to-door sales, we'll need professional sales people to make an effective sales pitch.

如果我们想要尝试挨户销售，我们必须请专业推销人员来介绍有效的推销技巧。

13. Why don't we do some comparative advertising? 我们为什么不能做一些对比广告呢?

14. Our product is definitely better than the competition's.

我们的产品肯定明显优于其他同类竞争产品。

15. We're advertising in every other media. It's high time we started placing ads on the Internet. 我们在其他媒介上都做广告，现在是我们开始在互联网上做广告的最佳时期了。

Listening

━━━━━ **Useful Expressions** ━━━━━

an ice-cream manufacturing company 冰激凌制造公司

marketing manager 市场营销经理　　marketing strategy 市场营销战略

marketing plan 市场营销计划书　　in good shape 完好无损

market opportunity 市场机会　　a good image 一个好的形象

marketing mix 市场营销组合　　customer relations 客户关系；客户关系部

point of view 观点　　clean up 打扫；〈口〉赚钱；整顿；痛打

department manager 部门经理，部门主管人

 Pair work：Listen to the dialogues and fill in the blanks.

━━━━━ Dialogue 1 ━━━━━

Marketing Strategy　　音频 5-1

In this conversation，Lily，the owner of an ice-cream manufacturing company，is talking with her marketing manager，Mary，about the marketing strategy for a new product.

Lily: So，Mary，do you have a _____ plan for our new ice-cream sandwich?

Mary: Yes，I do. After going _____ our S. W. O. T. process，I think we're in _____ _____ shape. One of our main strengths is the _____ of our ice-cream，and there is a good market _____ for the novelty of a choice of flavors. _____ our company already has a good image, I don't see many weaknesses. No other company _____ ice-cream sandwiches with a choice of 5 _____ , so there's no _____ ____ to speak of, either.

Lily: I assume we don't need to _____ creating a need, _____ summer almost here.

Mary: Right. As for the marketing _____ , we'll package it in gold foil with dark brown lettering to _____ chocolate, and price it 20% higher than our chocolate-covered ice-cream bar. It'll be _____ in selected places _____ the country _____ ____ next month. The main promotion will be through _____ , using a "pull" strategy, of course. We haven't _____ our ads yet, so I'll have to _____ you know. Can we _____ again in the beginning of next week?

Lily: Sure. Let me _____ , how about Tuesday morning at 10:30?

Mary: Uh, let's see, okay with me.

Lily: Alright. _____ , Mary. See you next week.

━━━━━ Dialogue 2 ━━━━━

Customer Issues

音频 5-2

In this conversation, Alice, head of Customer Relations for a large department store, is discussing some customer issues with Cao Ling, a staff member.

Alice: I called you in because I've been hearing about _____ many customer _____ _____ recently, even from some of our most _____ customers. What do you know _____ this, Cao Ling?

Cao Ling: We've had a lot of problems with certain items _____ a new manufacturer. We've handled it _____ the store policy of giving a _____ or an ____ _____ . Feedback from our _____ indicates some customers think our _____ control is lax.

Alice: From their _____ , they're right! It's not our _____ , of course, but what are we doing _____ it? Has there been any follow-up on this _____ ?

Cao Ling: We've contacted Purchasing, and they're dealing _____ the manufacturer right now.

Alice: That's not good _____ ! If we've had many complaints, let's get the __ _____ taken off the shelves until the manufacturer _____ their act.

Cao Ling: Alright. I'll talk to the _____ manager about it. Shouldn't be a problem, but it'll probably take them a day or two to _____ the empty space.

Alice: That's okay. Let's be proactive with the customers who bought those _____ _____. Send them a _____ for their next store purchase. And let's touch bases _____ our other recent customers to _____ that they're _____ with our customer policies.

Cao Ling: I'll get on it _____.

Alice: OK. Thanks, Cao Ling.

······ Part III   Practicing ·······

Reading

=== New Words and Phrases ===

boost [buːst] v. 增加；促进

revenue ['revənjuː] n. 收益；财政收入

highlight ['haɪlaɪt] n. 强调，突出

bonus ['bəʊnəs] n. 奖金，额外津贴

justify ['dʒstɪfaɪ] v. 证明……有理；为……辩护

checkout ['tʃekaʊt] n. 结账；检验

signage ['saɪnɪdʒ] n. 标记；标识系统

doorknob ['dɔːnɒb] n. 球形门把手

doormat ['dɔːmæt] n. 门前地垫

publicity [pʌb'lɪsəti] n. 宣传；公众信息

venue ['venjuː] n. 场地

notification [ˌnəʊtɪfɪ'keɪʃn] n. 通知；通知单；布告

circular ['sɜːkjələ(r)] adj. 圆形的；环行的；迂回的

terrific [tə'rɪfɪk] adj. 了不起的；极好的；异乎寻常的

bulletin board 公告牌

potential customers 潜在顾客

Work individually: Read the following passage and then paraphrase.

Promoting Your Sales Promotion

Sales promotions begin with the offer. That's especially true of one-time marketing concepts, such as you might use it to start or expand your small business, or to boost your short-term revenues. Your ideal promotional offer is something of value to your customers or clients, and *relevant* to your business, and *pertinent* to your competitive edge.

Sometimes, the easiest promotional offer is a discount, but often you can think of a smarter marketing idea if you try. What is your competitive edge? The single thing that sets you apart from your competition. How can your promotion highlight your competitive edge? Other common promotional offers include bonus products or services. Such promotions give customers a chance to "sample" your other products and services.

Once you have your promotional offer figured out, you must promote your sales promotion! This is why many small businesses fall short in their advertising and marketing efforts.

This failure happens in two ways.

First, they don't promote their promotion to their customers and potential customers.

Second, they communicate the wrong marketing message.

Let's examine the first one: *they don't promote their promotion to their customers and potential customers.*

When it comes to small business marketing, the first thought is usually advertising, but advertising adds expense. Between the cost of buying advertising media and the cost of the promotion itself, you may find that your returns don't justify the expense. In addition, advertising for a promotion tends to attract price-sensitive shoppers who may not return. There are smarter, cheaper ways to begin promoting your sales promotion, like a business owner reading a website called Tightwad Marketing. Here are a few specific marketing suggestions:

In-store
- In-store signage, especially at the entry, near relevant products, and at the checkout counter
- Have employees mention the promotion to all customers
- Employee buttons/tags/stickers that say "Ask me about (YOUR PROMOTION)"
- Reminders on receipts use an inexpensive rubber stamp or stickers
- Promotional flyer placed in bag at check-out

On-line
- Highlight your promotion on your website's main page
- Create a webpage about your promotion, and link to it from your main website page and your "What's New" section
- Collect email addresses from people who would like to receive promotional offers from your business

Telephone
- Have employees mention the promotion to callers
- Change your answering machine message to mention the promotion
- Mention and explain the promotion with your on-hold message
- Cold-call prospects either by location or market
- Call existing customers to inform them of this promotional opportunity

Flyer distribution
- Distribute to current customers, in-store or on-doorstep
- Include with mailed invoices, statements, or newsletters
- Include in bag at check-out
- Include in box with shipped merchandise
- Cross-promotion with other local businesses ("you distribute my promotional flyer and I'll distribute yours")

- Post on community bulletin boards，information boards，and other venues that permit such flyers
- Hand out flyers to passers-by
- Distribute door-to-door in targeted neighborhoods（NOTE：it's illegal to place anything in mailboxes，so you'll have to hang it from the doorknob，slip it into the door trim，or use the doormat to weigh down one edge）

Media

- Include an article about the promotion in your newsletter，if you have one
- Send out press releases to get publicity
- Permission-based email notification
- Postcards（cheap to create，cheap to mail）to existing customers
- Postcards to targeted potential customers
- Joint promotion with related businesses（"let's all chip in on a promotional marketing piece that we'll each distribute"）
- Okay，you also can advertise in your local shopping circular or newspaper．Classified advertisements are often a better deal than display advertising

In summary，get the word out to as many customers and potential customers as possible，as many ways as possible．You might have a terrific promotion，but without strong marketing support，no one will know about it，and it will fail．

Next，let's examine the second way many small businesses fall short in their promotional marketing efforts：*they communicate the wrong marketing message.*

If you think your message should be about your offer，believe it or not，you're wrong．Or，at least，not quite right enough to make your marketing efforts as effective as they could be．It's the mistake most business owners make，a mistake that's about to put you ahead of your competition because you're moments away from knowing better．

Your offer might be great to you，but the key to successfully promoting your promotion is to make your offer great to *your customer*．

In other words，your marketing message should be about *your customer*，and how he or she will benefit from your wonderful offer．

Speaking

New Words and Phrases

representative [ˌreprɪˈzentətɪv] *n.* 代表

cocktail [ˈkɒkteɪl] *n.* 鸡尾酒；混合物

martini [mɑːˈtiːni] *n.* （一杯）马丁尼酒

executive [ɪɡˈzekjətɪv] *n.* 总经理；行政部门

graphics [ˈɡræfɪks] *n.* 制图学；制图法；图表算法

workstation ['wɜːksteɪʃn] *n.* 工作站

powerful ['paʊəfl] *adj.* 强大的；权力大的

methodology [ˌmeθə'dɒlədʒi] *n.* 方法论；方法学

assumption [ə'sʌmpʃn] *n.* 承担；假定

rein [reɪn] *vi.* 严格控制

upgrade [ˌʌp'greɪd] *vi.* 提升；提高

foreseeable [fɔː'siːəbl] *adj.* 可预见到的

controversial [ˌkɒntrə'vɜːʃl] *adj.* 有争议的，引起争议的

arouse [ə'raʊz] *vt.* 引起；唤醒

affidavit [ˌæfə'deɪvɪt] *n.* 宣誓书

celebrity [sə'lebrəti] *n.* 名流；名声；名人

demographics [ˌdemə' græfɪks] *n.* 人口特征

segment ['segmənt] *n.* 环节；部分

brevity ['brevəti] *n.* 简洁；短暂

modifiable ['mɒdɪfaɪəbl] *adj.* 可更改的

guarantee [ˌgærən'tiː] *n.* 保证，担保

placement ['pleɪsmənt] *n.* 安置，放置

stated requirements 规定的要求

existing software 现有的软件

take full advantage of 充分利用

system combination 系统组合

a positive image 一个积极的形象

target customer 目标客户群

national footprint 国家的足迹

national presence 国家的存在

highlight strengths and benefits 突出优势和效益

in advance 提前；先期

market segmentation 市场分割；市场区割

graphical reproduction 图形再现

long life span 寿命长

repeat exposure to 重复暴露于

Pair work：Listen to the dialogues and have a role play.

音频 5－3

Dialogue 1

A Business Proposal

This conversation takes place during a business dinner.

Mark Davidson，a representative from a computer manufacturing company，is discussing a business proposal with Vicki Carmichael，the Purchasing Manager for a large IT firm.

Mark: Hello，Ms Carmichael. Please sit down. Would you like a cocktail?

Vicki: A dry martini，please. You can call me Vanessa. May I call you Mark?

Mark: Of course. Now，if you don't mind，Vanessa，I'd like to discuss some business before dinner. As the executive summary in my proposal shows，I think our new line of graphics workstations are exactly what you need. In fact，they're less expensive and more powerful than your stated requirements.

Vicki: No problem with that，Mark，but I question your objective of using a new operating system. That means new software and retraining.

Mark: Most of your existing software will work on the new system. The new software takes full advantage of our hardware and operating system combination，and will give your users the tools they need to increase productivity.

Vicki: I do like your proposed methodology of implementing in three phases. That's important for easing the impact to our users. Now, based on the assumption that they will need more power again in a few years, I need lots of expansion capability. Our capital expenditures on hardware and software have mushroomed over the last 5 years, and my CEO wants me to rein in our costs.

Mark: You'll be able to upgrade at relatively low cost to cover all your needs for the foreseeable future. Our hardware is very reliable, and the service contract gives you 24-hour on-location service for a full 3 years. Our growth impact studies show that cash flow expenditures over a 5-year period should be 35% less than other high-end workstations on the market.

Vicki: That's music to my ears, Mark. Looks like we can do business together. Cheers!

===== Dialogue 2 =====

音频 5 - 4

Advertising

Advertising is a paid-form of presentation or promotion of goods and services. It is non-personal in nature, and the promoter must be identified. Advertising's role is to create a positive image of a product or service by influencing the behavior of target customers.

When setting up an advertising campaign, you must make a choice on:

Form

National: advertising a copyrighted product or service across the national footprint. Identify brand name and emphasize national presence.

Retail: advertising by outlet emphasizing image and variety. Direct advertising directly to customers to avoid middlemen.

Advocacy: spreading that uses a perspective on a recognized controversial issue.

Style

Humorous: light-hearted.

Comparative: comparing one product to another, highlighting strengths and benefits over a competing product.

Emotional: creating a mood, arousing feelings, tring to meet psychological needs.

Lifestyle: associating brand/product/service with the way people live and work.

Testimonial: affidavit of support by a customer or celebrity.

Reason why: touting the benefit and necessity of a product to avoid adverse situations.

Slice of life: typically focusing on an average family and everyday or common setting.

Media

Television: most expensive, audio-visual impact, reaching a mass audience, easily and effectively targeted based on well-known viewer demographics.

Newspaper: most widely used medium, rapid and flexible coverage, ads easily changed, less expensive than television. Short attention span, poor reproduction quality, usually no color, not easily targeted.

Direct mail: less expensive than TV or newspaper but higher advance costs, audience easily selected, demographics of percentage of serious recipients can be predicted in advance.

Radio: fairly inexpensive, mass audience, audiences are largely segmented and easily targeted. Only audio, brevity doesn't allow for educating viewers about complex products, audience less attentive.

Magazine: relatively inexpensive, huge variety provides a high level of market segmentation, lots of space for detailed product information, excellent graphical reproduction, long life span, repeat exposure to multiple readers. Not quickly modifiable, long lead time before printing, no guarantee of placement within the magazine.

Outdoor: inexpensive, little competition for customer attention, high repeat exposure. Limited information, little control over target audience.

Internet: potential mass audience, but no control and little targeting capability. Difficult to control reader's attention, some delivery problems.

Module 2

Human Resources Management Situation

Unit 6 Recruitment and Selecting

━━━━ Objectives ━━━━

In this unit, the students are required to grasp the following contents.

1. Learning to talk something about recruitment and selecting with some given useful words and phrases of this unit freely.

2. Learning to talk something about recruitment and selecting with some given useful sentences of this unit freely.

3. Reading a passage about recruitment and selecting and then paraphrasing it.

4. Listening and having a role play about recruitment and selecting.

······ Part I   Preparing ······

 Work individually: What questions will you be asked in your interview?

In your interview, you will be asked...	Often	Sometimes	Never
What have you enjoyed most about working here?			
What skills and experiences would make an ideal candidate?			
How does this job fit into your career plan?			
Why did you apply for this job?			
What are your strengths?			
Why should we hire you?			

 Pair work: Compare your answers with a partner.

I have never been interviewed, especially in school. What about you?

······· Part II　Performing ·······

Reading

=============== New Words and Phrases ===============

admin. administrative 行政的

Jr. junior 初级

agcy. agency 经销商

knowl. knowledge 知识

appt. appointment 约会；预约

loc. location 位置；场所

asst. assistant 助理

lv/lvl. level 级/层

attn. attention 给，与……联系

mach. machine 机器

bkgd. background 背景

bus. business 商业；生意

mgr. manager 经理

clk. clerk（办公室）职员

co. company 公司

coll. college 大专（学历）

comm. commission 佣金

corp. corporation（有限）公司

ot. overtime 超时

dept. department 部

pls. please 请

dir. director 董事

pos. position 职位

div. division 分工；部门

pref. preference（有经验者）优先

prev. previous 有先前（经验）

eves. evenings 晚上

refs. references 推荐信

exc. excellent 很好的

rel. reliable 可靠的

exp. experience 经验

reps. representative（销售）代表

exp'd. experienced 有经验的

sal. salary 工资

secty. secretary 秘书

wk. week/work 周/工作

sr. senior 资深

stmts. statements 报告

hqtrs. headquarters 总部

tech. technical 技术上

hr. hour 小时

tel. /ph. telphone 电话

hrly. hourly 每小时

temp. temporarily 临时性（工作）

trans. transportation 交通

immed. immediate 立即

trnee. trainee 实习生

typ. typing/typist 打字/打字员

data. pro data processing 数据处理

m-f. monday-friday 从周一到周五

HS. high school 高中（学历）

wpm. words per minute 打字/每分钟

etc. and so on 等等

P/T. part time 非全日制

F/T. full time 全日制

fr. ben fringe benefits 额外福利

Group work：Read the following sentences and learn how to use them freely.

Personal information introduction

1. My name is... 我是……

2. I'm from... 我来自……

3. My birthplace / hometown is... 我的家乡是……

4. My native place is... 我的籍贯是……

5. I'm a native here. 我是本地人。

6. I believe my academic record proves that I am a steady, diligent, imaginative and thorough worker.
   我相信我在学校的记录能证明我是一个稳重踏实、勤勉、富有想象力而且认真的员工。

Educational background

1. I obtained / received my bachelor degree from... university.
   我从……大学获得了学士学位。

2. I majored in Chemistry. 我是学化学专业的。

3. I graduated from Renmin Business School at People's University of China.
   我毕业于中国人民大学商学院。

4. I've learned Economics there for four years. 我在那里学了 4 年经济学。

5. I passed college English Test Band-4/6, with good skill in listening, speaking, reading and writing. 我通过了大学英语四级、六级考试，有良好的英语听说读写能力。

Personal abilities

1. I manage my time well. 我很懂得分配时间。

2. I suppose a strong point is that I like developing new things and ideas.
   我想我有一个优点就是喜欢创新。

3. When I think something is right, I will stick to that.
   若我认为某件事是对的，我会坚持到底。

4. I stick to my principles and keep to the rules. 我会坚持原则，谨守规则。

5. I know effective ways of doing sth. 我知道做某事的有效方法。

6. I am experienced / proficient in doing sth. 我熟练掌握某事。

7. I feel capable of doing sth. 我有能力做某事。

8. I'm pretty good at /proficient in / quite efficient in sth. 我在……方面很出色。

9. I have a clear idea of how the international trade works. 我对国际贸易如何运作了如指掌。

10. I think I can manage. 我认为我能行。

Working experience

1. I started as an office clerk, and became a department manager three years later. About two years ago, I was appointed as an assistant to the general manager. 我从办公室职员做起，三年后成了一名部门经理。大约在两年前，我被任命为总经理助理。

2. I established business ties with several firms. 我和几个公司建立了业务关系。

3. I worked for a foreign company as a manager. 我在一家外企担任经理。

Personal achievements

1. As a marketing manager，I managed to rise our products' share from 30％ to 40％ in Southwest China.

   作为销售经理，我成功地把我们的产品在西南地区所占的市场份额从30％提高到40％。

2. I succeeded in increasing the annual turnover. 我成功地提高了年营业额。

3. I have reduced our administration cost by 15％. 我把管理成本减少了15％。

4. I succeeded in promoting our products to America and Canada.

   我将公司产品成功地推广到了美国和加拿大。

Personalities

1. I am a curious person，and I like to learn new things.

   我是一个充满好奇心的人，而且喜欢学习新的事物。

2. I'd like to be thought of as someone who can be trusted.

   我喜欢被当作可以信赖的人来看待。

3. I think I'm reasonably cheerful by nature. 我认为我的性格相当开朗。

4. Frankly speaking，I think I'm honest and reliable. 坦率地讲，我认为我诚实可靠。

5. I think I'm initiative and responsible in doing things. 我认为我做事主动，富有责任心。

6. I feel I can think independently and work cooperatively.

   我认为我能独立思考并能与人合作。

7. I think I'm easy to approach and friendly to everyone.

   我认为我很容易接近，对人也很友好。

8. I think I have an inquiring mind，and I like to ask why.

   我认为我爱思考，总爱问为什么。

9. Time is money and efficiency is life. Whatever I do，I always seize the day and attach importance to efficiency.

   时间就是金钱，效率就是生命。不管我做什么，我总是抓紧时间，注重效率。

Listening 🎧

Useful Expressions

copy of resume 简历副本　　　　　　　　　in the education field 在教育领域

nothing less than 不超过　　　　　　　　　educational background 教育背景

analytical and interpersonal skills 分析能力和人际关系技巧

job description 工作描述　　　　　　　　　computer programmer 计算机程序员

system analysis 系统分析　　　　　　　　　software support 软件支持

Opportunity knocks. 成功的机会来了。　　　academic background 学术背景

Pair work：Listen to the dialogues and fill in the blanks.

音频 6 - 1

━━━━ **Dialogue 1** ━━━━

Interview（1）

A: What experience do you _____ for this kind of job?

B: Here is a copy of my resume. Please _____.

A: How long have you been at your present place of _____?

B: I have fifteen years _____ in the _____. I am looking for a job more _____ to my _____ and that can satisfy my _____ to be constantly challenged.

A: What salary _____ do you have?

B: _____ six figures.

A: Tell me about your _____.

B: I graduated from _____ with honors.

━━━━ **Dialogue 2** ━━━━

Interview（2）

音频 6 - 2

Q: Can you sell _____ in two minutes? _____ it.

A: With my _____ and experience, I feel I am hardworking, _____ and _____ in any project I undertake. Your organization could _____ from my analytical and _____.

Q: Give me a _____ of your current job description.

A: I have been working as a _____ for five years. To be specific, I do _____, trouble shooting and provide _____ support.

Q: Why did you leave your _____?

A: Well，I am hoping to get an _____ of a better position. If _____ knocks，I will take it.

Q: How do you _____ yourself as a professional?

A: With my strong _____, I am capable and _____.

Q: What contribution did you make to your current（previous）_____?

A: I have finished three new _____, and I am sure I can apply my experience to this _____.

Q: What do you think you are _____ to us?

A: I feel I can make some _____ contributions to your company _____.

Q: What makes you think you would be a _____ in this position?

A: My graduate school training combined with my _____ should qualify me for this _____ job. I am sure I will be successful.

Q: Do you work well under _____ or _____?

A: The trait is needed in my _____ (previous) position and I know I can _____ it well.

· · · · · · · **Part III　Practicing** · · · · · · ·

Reading

==== New Words and Phrases ====

candidate ['kændɪdət] *n.* 申请求职者

relationship [rɪ'leɪʃnʃɪp] *n.* 关系；联系

positive ['pɒzətɪv] *adj.* 积极的；确实的

negative ['negətɪv] *adj.* 消极的；否认的

prospective [prə'spektɪv] *adj.* 未来的；预期的

bureaucratic [ˌbjʊərə'krætɪk] *adj.* 官僚的，官僚主义的，官僚作风的

conscientious [ˌkɒnʃɪ'enʃəs] *adj.* 认真负责的；本着良心的；谨慎的；正大光明的

crisper ['krɪspə] *adj.* 新奇的

inspiration [ˌɪnspə'reɪʃn] *n.* 灵感

carry out 进行；执行；完成

one-to-one 一一对应的；一对一的

build up 逐步建立；增进

at ease 安逸，自由自在；自然；心净

certain area 某些地区

turn into 成为；（使）变成；译成

mutual interest 相互利益

on the basis of 根据；依据；以……为基础；按照

be altered to 被改变为……

Work individually：Read the following passage and then paraphrase.

Types of Interview

Interviews may be carried out in a one-to-one situation; or a group of interviewers may interview a single candidate; or a single interviewer may interview a group of candidates. Each type of interviewer has its advantages and disadvantages.

The one-to-one interview is the most common. It has the advantage of being the most natural situation. It is easier to build up a relationship with the candidate; he will feel at ease and will answer questions more fully and more naturally. In particular he will be in a good position to find out whether or not he would want the candidate to work with him or under him. These advantages carry with them certain disadvantages. The interviewer may be so strongly affected by his own positive or negative feelings that he is unable to assess the candidate fairly. The interview may be so relaxed that the interviewer forgets to explore certain areas; it may turn into a conversation about topics of mutual interest. The candidate himself or the interviewer's organization is likely to feel that the procedure is somewhat unfair; a prospective employee ought not to be accepted or rejected on the basis of an interview with just one person. And of course, unless the interviewer is highly skilled, the candidate and organization are right — because the best people are not necessarily going to be selected. The procedure might then be altered to include additional one-to-one interviews.

The next most common type of interview is the board interview. This is usually adopted by larger bureaucratic organization in order that the selection procedure shall be seen to be fairer to candidates and so that people who are selected reach some kind of common standard. It also has some other advantages. A board may be more conscientious in covering all relevant areas simply because members keep a critical eye on one another. They may also be more careful in reaching a decision based on all the available evidence. Often the questioning in a board interview is crisper and more relevant — partly because of the critical presence of other board members and partly because when any particular board member loses inspiration, another can take over. Also an inexperienced member can learn from others about questions to ask and standards to use.

Speaking

=== New Words and Phrases ===

colleague [ˈkɒliːg] n. 同事；同行；同僚
institute [ˈɪnstɪtjuːt] n. 学院；协会；学会
secretary [ˈsekrətri] n. 秘书；干事
pressure [ˈpreʃə(r)] n. 压力
administrative [ədˈmɪnɪstrətɪv] adj. 管理的，行政的
job seekers 求职者

graduate from 毕业于……，从……毕业
Shenzhen Institute of Information Technology 深圳信息职业技术学院
administrative management 行政管理
training program 训练方案
get along with 进展；与……和睦相处
be familiar with 对……熟悉

 Pair work: Listen to the dialogues and have a role play.

=== Dialogue 1 ===

A Group Interview Conversation

There are four job seekers knocking at the door.

音频 6-3

Mr. Lin: Come in, please. Please take a seat. Well, let's begin.

Mr. Wu: OK, we're interviewers. I'm Mr. Wu. They are my colleagues — Mr. Lin and Miss Fan. (Mr. Lin and Miss Fan smile and nod their heads)

Miss Fan: Glad to meet you. Please introduce yourselves. From left to right.

Miss Wei: Hello. My name is Manru Wei. I graduated from Shenzhen Institute of Information Technology. My major is secretary and I am 21 years old.

Miss Chen: Good morning. I'm Yilin Chen. I majored in administrative management and graduated from Shenzhen University this year. I am 20 years old.

Mr. Zhang: My name is Junyi Zhang and I'm 21 years old. I graduated from Zhongshan University. I majored in secretary.

Miss Zhou: I graduated from Shenzhen Institute of Information Technology this year. I majored in secretary.

Dialogue 2

One-to-one Interview Conversation

音频 6 - 4

A: Why are you interested in working for our company?

B: Because your operations are global, so I feel I can gain the most from working in this kind of environment. And I'm very interested in your company's training program.

A: What are your great strengths?

B: I'm a fast-learner. And I can work under pressure and get along with my colleagues.

A: In what specific ways will our company benefit from hiring you?

B: I have enough knowledge to market the products of your company. So I'm very familiar with this market and have many customers. I think your company will benefit from it.

A: What are your salary expectations?

B: Shall we discuss my responsibilities with your company first? I think salary is closely related to the responsibilities of the job. I expect to be paid according to my abilities.

A: We'll inform you when we've made our decision. Thanks for coming.

B: OK.

Unit 7 Employee Training and Staff Performance Appraisal

═══ Objectives ═══

In this unit, the students are required to grasp the following contents.

1. Learning to talk something about employee training and staff performance appraisal with some given useful words and phrases of this unit freely.

2. Learning to talk something about employee training and staff performance appraisal with some given useful sentences of this unit freely.

3. Reading a passage about employee training and then paraphrasing it.

4. Listening and having a role play about employee training.

······ **Part I   Preparing** ······

 Work individually: What contents does the employee training include?

About employee training	Often	Sometimes	Never
Staff training			
Training needs analysis			
Training approaches			
Evaluating the training needs			
Implementation of staff training procedures			
Assessing the effectiveness of training			
Strategic training			

 Pair work: Compare your answers with a partner.

I have never been trained, especially in our unit. What about you?

⋯⋯⋯ **Part II　Performing** ⋯⋯⋯

Reading

===== New Words and Phrases =====

executive [ɪˈgzekjutɪv] *n.* 高级管理人员

profession [prəˈfeʃn] *n.* 职业

ethics [ˈeθɪks] *n.* 道德标准

specialist [ˈspeʃəlɪst] *n.* 专家

policy [ˈpɒləsi] *n.* 政策

mission [ˈmɪʃn] *n.* 使命；任务

aiming [ˈeɪmɪŋ] *n.* 准确度

selection [sɪˈlekʃn] *n.* 选择

shareholder [ˈʃeəhəʊldə(r)] *n.* 股东

selection rate 入选率

cutoff score 录用分数线

job knowledge test 业务知识测试

employment interview 求职面试

unstructured interview 非结构化面试

structured interview 结构化面试

group interview 小组面试

vocational interest test 职业兴趣测试

board interview 会议型面试

business games 经营管理策略

case study 案例研究

conference method 会议方法

role playing 角色扮演

job rotating 工作轮换

on-the-job training (OJT) 在职培训

external environment 外部环境

internal environment 内部环境

informal organization 非正式组织

multinational corporation (MNC) 跨国公司

managing diversity 管理多样性

human resource management (HRM) 人力资源管理

human resource manager 人力资源经理

operative employees 操作工

the Human Resource Certification Institute (HRCI) 人力资源认证协会

through thick and thin 不畏艰险；在任何情况下

 Group work：Read the following sentences and learn how to use them freely.

1. Is your performance review just around the corner? There's no need to panic but now would be a good time to prepare.

   你的绩效考核是不是即将来临了？没有必要慌张，但现在就该开始准备了。

2. Experts offer these tips for making your review go more smoothly.

   下面是专家们提供的建议，让你的考核进行得更顺利。

3. Dust off your previous review. 重提上次的考核。

4. If you had a review at this company a year ago, it probably contains a list of goals. Ideally, you will have been working on these goals this year. 如果你去年有过一次绩效考核，可能其中就会包含一系列目标。理想的情况下，今年你会一直在实现这些目标。

5. Often, however, you'll realize something has changed. Perhaps a new boss gave you a new direction, or the project you were supposed to focus on got delayed. Richard Phillips, a career coach and owner of Advantage Career Solutions, recommends making sure you have documentation for changes such as these, in case there's a question at review time.

不过往往你会发现事情已经起了变化。也许新老板给你一个新的工作方向，或你本来要致力的项目被推迟。优势职业方案的老板和职业教练理查德·菲利普斯建议人们一定要记录下这些变化，以防考核时出现疑问。

6. What if your boss never officially told you that your goals had changed, but instead just kept piling on other work so that you weren't able to start the projects you discussed at your last review? It would have been best to bring this up with your boss when it happened. 万一你的老板没有正式通知你的目标已经改变，而只是增加你的工作量，从而使你无法开始上一次考核定下的项目，这该怎么办？最好在当初（老板安排别的工作时）就提出这个问题。

7. If you didn't, however, it's important to frame your actions the right way. "Say at review time, 'I made a strategic decision that this needed more of my attention than that,'" Phillips said. "Don't make it sound like you just forgot or you blew it off."

如果你没这么做，那么谈论你工作的方式就很重要。菲利普斯建议，"考核的时候可以这样说，'我做出了一个策略上的决定，这项工作比那项更需要关注'。别听上去像是你忘记了或你办糟了。"

8. I am writing to follow up on our earlier decision on the marketing campaign in Q2.
我写信来跟进我们之前对于第二季度营销活动的决定。

9. Your patience with another person may wear thin if he keeps doing something you don't like. 要是一个人老是做你不喜欢的事，那你对他就会越来越没有耐心。

10. spread too thin 同时做太多事情

Listening 🎧

======= **Useful Expressions** =======

staff training 员工培训	stop fussing 别大惊小怪
get together 聚会；联欢；收集；整理	corporate culture 企业文化
fit into 适应，适合	office secretary 办公室秘书
be essential to 对……来说至关重要	working hours 工作时间
employee card 员工卡	alphabetical order 字母顺序
keep in mind 记住	be cautious about 对……谨慎

Pair work：Listen to the dialogues and fill in the blanks.

音频 7 - 1

=== Dialogue 1 ===

Staff Training（1）

Cheney: The _____ of my _____ is over. But I heard that our company will hold _____ staff training.

Bertha: Stop fussing！I think the _____ is very necessary for our newcomers. And my company also tells me to _____ the training next week.

Cheney: I suppose that the training will be boring. A group of strangers _____ and listen to those _____ speeches.

Bertha: I don't agree _____ you. It is said that the leaders of our company held a _____ about the in-service _____. They decided to make a _____ plan for staff training, so as to _____ the training effects. Through the training, we should know that the _____ and spirit are the most important things in a company. Our newcomers can really grasp the _____ of the corporate culture and _____. So the new staff can fit into our company and do jobs well.

Cheney: Well，I _____ the meaning of the training now. Besides, I can get along with some new colleagues in Chenxing Company.

Bertha: That's right. From the _____ we can know _____ them and the company.

Cheney: Well，well，well，I am hungry now. Shall we _____ this evening?

Bertha: I am _____ now. Here we go.

=== Dialogue 2 ===

Staff Training（2）

音频 7 - 2

Sparks: Bertha，morning.

Bertha: Morning，Madam.

Sparks: You are going to work as my _____ from next Monday. Right now I want to _____ you the rules of our company.

Bertha: Thank you for your _____. The rules are also _____ me to know more about ACD Company.

Sparks: The working hours are from 8：30 to 11：30 in the morning and from 1：30 to 6：30 in the afternoon. _____ never to be late or _____. Every time you should use the _____ to show you are present whenever you _____ into the company.

Bertha: I will do my duty.

Sparks: _____, a secretary must _____ office routine and try to do something by yourself.

Bertha: That's true. I will _____ to do whatever I am given.

Sparks: Bertha, please _____me. This is the filing cabinet and any _____ or file you need can be found here.

Bertha: I understand this. Would you like me to _____ them according to dates?

Sparks: I don't think so. You should file them in alphabetical _____. And here is a safe. The _____ files are kept here. I will give you the _____ to the safe later. But you must _____ that you have to _____ this.

Bertha: Yes, I will.

Sparks: Last thing I want to show you is to _____these files. Don't be ____ _____.

Bertha: OK. I'll keep all these in _____. Thanks a lot for what you told me.

······ Part III   Practicing ······

Reading ✎

▬▬ New Words and Phrases ▬▬

survey ['sɜːvei] n. 调查；勘测

productivity [ˌprɒdʌk'tɪvəti] n. 生产率，生产力

flexibility ['fleksə'bɪləti] n. 柔度；柔韧性，机动性

morale ['mɒrəl] n. 士气；精神面貌

responsiveness [rɪ'spɒnsɪvnəs] n. 响应性，易起反应

workshop ['wɜːkʃɒp] n. 车间；专题讨论会，研究会

presentation [ˌprezn'teɪʃn] n. 提交；演出；

陈述，报告；颁奖仪式

seminar ['semɪnɑː] n. 研讨会；研讨班，讲习会；研讨小组

consequence ['kɒnsɪkwəns] n. 推论；结果，成果

commitment [kə'mɪtmənt] n. 承诺，许诺；委任，委托

insurance premiums 保险费

retention rate 保留率

frankly speaking 坦率地讲

finger out 想出

 Work individually： Read the following passage and then paraphrase.

The Benefits of Staff Training

According to studies and surveys, the following are the good results of staff training：

* Improved quality of work

* Increased productivity

* Greater flexibility and responsiveness to change

* Reduced insurance premiums

* Less wastage

* Reduced maintenance and repair costs

* Greater commitment from staff

* Higher staff retention rate

* Improved morale

Helping the staff to develop through trainings is the best and greatest contribution an organization can make to their well-being. When the trainings are well done, the reward will be many times over the invested time, effort and money. The results to these trainings productivity, efficiency and job satisfaction are sure guarantees to the success of the organization. I will present three points on staff training—the importance, methods and effectiveness.

For the first point, it's important for a company to organize training for their employees.

Firstly, it's a way to make the new recruit to be familiar with the background and the task they should take.

Secondly, the professional training can make progress on staff quality. It will achieve the further outcome for the company.

Thirdly, it will motivate the workers' loyalty. Therefore, it's necessary for a company to give staff training.

For the second point—methods, what methods can be used to give staff training? I think there are mounts of ways, for example, the workshop, presentation, seminar, the meeting and so on. It's better to combine all of these methods together and make the training regularly.

For the third point—effectiveness, when we organize training, how can we identify its result? Does it really work? Frankly speaking, some consequence cannot be seen by eyes such as the motivation influence. But we still have some methods to assess the activity. One method is to analysis the sales data and study the take-over rate. The two researches can tell us the final result.

From above mentioned, we can now conclude that staff training plays an important role in the development of a company. And we can also finger out some methods to be used on staff training. What's more, we also should see the feedback of the training to adjust it better.

Perhaps topping the list of the benefits is that often overlooked fact that staff skills are recognized through these trainings, and they feel that they are being valued by the company.

Speaking 🎤

================= New Words and Phrases =================

administer [əd'mɪnɪstə(r)] *n.* 管理者

arbitration [ˌɑːbɪ'treɪʃn] *n.* 仲裁

strike [straɪk] *n.* 罢工

discipline ['dɪsəplɪn] *n.* 纪律

grievance ['griːvəns] *n.* 申诉

demotion [ˌdiː'məʊʃn] *n.* 降职

transfer ['trænsfɜː(r)] *n.* 调动

annuity [ə'njuːəti] *n.* 退休金

pension ['penʃn] *n.* 退休金

absenteeism [ˌæbsən'tiːɪzəm] *n.* 缺勤

ability test 能力测试

ability of manager 管理者的能力

absence management 缺勤管理

craft union 行业工会

industrial union 产业工会

national union 全国工会

bargaining union 谈判组

collective bargaining 劳资谈判

internal employee relations 内部员工关系

disciplinary action 纪律处分

absent with leave 因故缺勤；（被）许可缺勤

absent without leave 无故缺勤，擅离职守

accelerating premium 累进奖金制

accident frequency 事故频率

accident insurance 意外伤害保险

accident investigation 事故调查

accident loss 事故损失

accident work injury 工伤事故

achievement need 成就需求

achievement test 成就测试

action learning 行动（行为）学习法

action research 行动（行为）研究

administrative level 管理层次

administrative line 直线式管理

alternative dispute resolution（ADR）建设性
　　争议解决方法

adventure learning 探险学习法

adverse impact 负面影响

affiliation need 归属需求

age composition 年龄结构

annual bonus 年终分红

annual leave 年假

application blank 申请表

appraisal feedback 考评反馈

appraisal interview 考评面谈

appraisal standardization 考评标准化

appraiser training 考评者培训

apprenticeship training 学徒式培训

career anchors 职业锚，职业动机

career counseling 职业咨询

career cycle 职业周期

career development method 职业发展方法

career path 职业途径

career planning 职业规划

career stage 职业阶段

Pair work：Listen to the dialogues and have a role play.

音频 7 - 3

 Dialogue 1

Training Program（1）

A: Now I'd like to explain your training program to you.

B: How long will the program be?

A: About three weeks. In the first week, you will learn about our products, marketing strategy and the information of our competitors.

B: Oh, that will be very interesting. What about the second week?

A: In the second and the third week, you will work with an experienced salesman and watch how he deals with the customers. After that, you need to write a training report as a conclusion.

B: Well, I haven't expected that I need to write a report. I think the training will be useful to my future work.

 Dialogue 2

Training Program（2）

A: Are you ready to have the on-the-job training?

B: Yes. I can't wait to know what kind of job I will do.

A: As a project assistant, you need to look for the information of potential customers and call them. If you can get an appointment with that company, you should report to your manager.

B: I see. That's too difficult. I guess I will have a lot of appointments.

A: Good. Then it is you who need to contact with those companies and try to do business with them.

B: What will I do if I come into some problem?

A: You can ask those experienced colleagues and consult your boss. I am sure they will be ready to help you. When the business is almost done, you need to prepare the contract.

B: Will I work alone and do all of the things by myself?

A: Of course not. If it is a big deal, a lot of people will do it together. And there are four people in the project department, so you will work with them.

Module

3

Etiquette Situation

Unit 8 Telephone Etiquette

In this unit, the students are required to grasp the following contents.

1. Learning to talk something about telephone etiquette with some given useful words and phrases of this unit freely.

2. Learning to talk something about telephone etiquette with some given useful sentences of this unit freely.

3. Reading a passage about telephone etiquette and then paraphrasing it.

4. Listening and having a role play about telephone etiquette.

······· Part I   Preparing ·······

 Work individually: What do you usually do when you make a phone call?

Make a phone call, you like to...	Often	Sometimes	Never
make a phone call in a private room			
speak loudly in public place			
tell the other person your company and your name when your phone is answered			
confirm it is the right person you want to speak to			
apologize after dialling the wrong number			
hold on till the other person hangs up			

 Pair work: Compare your answers with a partner.

Have you dialled your private number by office telephone?

Module 3 Etiquette Situation

Part II Performing

Reading

New Words and Phrases

cast [kɑːst] *vt.* 通过

screen [skriːn] *v.* 筛选

identified [aɪ'dentɪfaɪd] *v.* 确认；辨认；认出；支持

threatening ['θretnɪŋ] *adj.* 胁迫的；险恶的；要变坏的

barrier ['bærɪə] *n.* 屏障；障碍；栅栏；分界线

rude [ruːd] *adj.* 粗鲁的；简陋的；狂暴的；近乎下流的

prescription [prɪs'krɪpʃən] *n.* 处方药；[医] 药方，处方；指示；法规

apologize [ə'pɒlədʒaɪz] *v.* 道歉，认错；辩解，辩护

underestimate [ˌʌndər'estɪmeɪt] *v.* 低估；对……估计不足

interrupted [ɪntə'rʌptɪd] *adj.* 中断的；被遮断的；被阻止的；不通的

initial [ɪ'nɪʃəl] *adj.* 最初的；开始的；首字母的

listener ['lɪsənə] *n.* 听众，倾听者

original [ə'rɪdʒənl] *adj.* 原始的；最初的

insurance [ɪn'ʃuərəns] *n.* 保险费；保险，保险业

polite [pə'laɪt] *adj.* 客气的，有礼貌的

etiquette ['etɪ'ket] *n.* 礼仪，礼节；规矩；礼数

offend [ə'fend] *v.* 触怒；得罪，冒犯；使反感，令人不适

pity ['pɪtɪ] *n.* 怜悯；同情；可惜的事；憾事

take a call 接电话

excuse me 不好意思，对不起

Hold on/One moment, please! 请稍等。

Sorry, his/her line is busy. 对不起，正在占线。

Would you like to leave a message? 你想留言吗？

🌸 Group work：Read the following sentences and learn how to use them freely.

1. I've really got to go，I'll call back to you when I get the office.
   我真的得走了，我到办公室再打给你。

2. Sorry，I must end the conversation．There's someone on the other line.
   抱歉，我不能再说了。我还有另外一通电话要接。

3. I think I'd better let you go．I'll talk to you later.
   我想我应该让你去忙了，我晚点再打给你。

4. I have to get back to work．I'll call you later tonight.
   我要回去工作了。我今晚再打给你。

57

5. Shall we continue this later? I've got a call waiting.

   我们可不可以晚一点再继续聊? 我这边有个电话打进来了。

6. It's kind of late. Why don't we talk about it tomorrow? 有点晚了。我们何不明天再谈呢?

7. I've got to meet a client right now. Can we talk later?

   我现在要去见一个客户。我们可以晚一点再谈吗?

8. I won't keep you any longer. 我不耽误你的时间了。

9. Sorry, it's getting late. Can you call again tomorrow morning?

   抱歉,时候不早了。你可不可以明天早上再打来?

10. I'm sorry, I don't speak English well. I'll have an English speaker call you back later.
    May I have your name and telephone number? 很抱歉,我英语说得不好。我找位会讲英
    语的人稍后回电话给你。请教您的大名及电话号码?

Listening

══ Useful Expressions ══

sales department 销售部   speak to 跟⋯⋯讲话   hold the line 稍等

discuss with 和⋯⋯商量   sign contract 签合同

IBM Computer Company IBM 电脑公司   managing director 常务董事; 总经理

Pair work: Listen to the dialogues and fill in the blanks.

音频 8-1

══ Dialogue 1 ══

Leave a Message

A: Good afternoon, Sales _____. May I help you?

B: Could I _____ to Mr. Bush, please?

A: I'll see if he is _____. Who shall I say is _____, please?

B: John Smith.

A: _____ the line, please. Mr. Bush is in a meeting with the Managing Director at
the _____, I'm afraid. Can I _____ you?

B: Well, I want to _____ with him the new contract we _____ last week.

A: I don't think the meeting will go on much longer. Shall I ask him to call you when he is __
_____ ?

B: Yes, that would be easiest.

音频 8 - 2

Dialogue 2

Introduction

A: Stone Corp. Hi, Mary _____.

B: Hello, I'd like to _____ to Mr. Hunter, please.

A: May I ask who is calling, please?

B: My name is Herbert Wood of IBM Computer Company.

A: Thank you, Mr. Wood. One _____, please...

C: Can you find _____ what he wants?

A: Yes, Mr. Hunter. I'm sorry to have _____ you waiting, Mr. Wood. Mr. Hunter is rather _____ right now and would like to know what you wish to speak to him about.

B: Yes, I want to buy some computer software and talk about developing some other software. I don't know whether he is _____ in that or not?

A: I see. Thank you very much, Mr. Wood. Would you _____ a moment, please?

C: I see. Put him on _____ two.

A: Yes, Mr. Hunter. Mr. Wood, I'm very sorry to have kept you waiting. I'll put you _____ to Mr. Hunter.

······ Part III   Practicing ······

Reading

New Words and Phrases

cognitive ['kɒgnɪtɪv] *adj.* 认知的；认识的

vibrate ['vaɪbreɪt] *v.* 振动；摆动；犹豫；激动

engage [ɪn'geɪdʒ] *v.* 从事

relevant ['relɪvənt] *v.* 聘用；吸引住

urge [ɜːdʒ] *n.* 强烈的欲望

interrupt [ɪntə'rʌpt] *v.* 打断（别人的话等）；阻止；截断

effectively [ɪ'fektɪvli] *adv.* 有效地；实际上

delay [dɪ'leɪ] *n.* 耽搁；延迟，拖延

impression [ɪm'preʃən] *n.* 印象，感觉；影

响，效果

disrespect [dɪsrɪ'spekt] *n.* 失礼，无礼

cafeteria [ˌkæfə'tɪərɪə] *n.* 自助餐厅

grab [græb] *n.* 抓住

pad [pæd] *n.* 便签本

answer ['ɑːnsə(r)] *v.* 接电话

substitute ['sʌbstɪtjuːt] *v.* 代替

an amazingly useful machine 非常有用的机器

on vibrate 震动

training sessions 培训课程，培训会

59

personal texting 个人短信

turn away from 把脸从……转过去

make a positive impression 留下一个积极的印象

relevant contact information 相关联系信息

 **Work individually**：Read the following passage and then paraphrase.

The telephone is an amazingly useful machine, and very easy to use, but believe it or not, people don't always use them effectively. Because we're busy and focused on ourselves, we often use our phones in a manner that is helpful for us, but not necessarily for everyone else.

Hopefully you know a few of the basics, such as keeping your phone volume low, or on vibrate, resisting the urge to use them during meetings or training sessions, and of course, refraining from personal texting while at work. For personal texting, it's best to give yourself one or two times per day. You'll step away from your work outside, or in a cafeteria, and then engage your personal texts.

Those are obviously important, but what I really want you to think about is how you interact and respect the person with whom you're speaking. And that begins before you even pick up the phone. When you hear the ring, grab a pad of paper and pen, so you can be ready to take needed notes without causing a delay while you look around your desk. Before saying "hello" I want you to smile, and choose to be positive. How you feel will be sensed by the person on the other end of the phone, so smile and make a positive impression.

Right after you say "hello", be sure you've turned away from your computer towards the area of your office least likely to be distracting. No multitasking of any kind allowed—in fact, just looking at your pad of paper and pen is a really good idea, because it encourages cognitive focus. Next, if the call isn't for you, but is for someone else in the department or company, don't say he dialed the wrong number; don't say he did anything wrong at all. Instead, help him. Connect him to the person, or at least share relevant contact information.

Finally, during the call, remember to never interrupt the person. Interrupting tends to be viewed by everyone as a sign of disrespect. If you're very busy and facing a huge deadline, you can shape the call when it's your turn to speak, for example, by telling them you need to get back to them, but then, do suggest a specific time. Of course, if you're honestly not able to talk, you probably shouldn't have answered the call, unless it's your boss, or a person you're expecting an important call from.

The telephone is your friend, but if you don't use it correctly, it won't necessarily make you look friendly. Remember the tips above, and you'll connect successfully by building only positive impressions.

Speaking

─── New Words and Phrases ───

market department 市场部

secretary of president 主席的秘书

sale department 贩卖部，营业部

in the conference room 在会议室

dropping sales 销售下降

Pair work：Listen to the dialogues and have a role play.

─── Dialogue 1 ───

What Can I Do for You?

音频 8 - 3

A: Good morning，this is market department. What can I do for you?

B: Good morning，I am the secretary of president. Can I speak to Mr. Black?

A: I'm afraid our manager is not available at the moment. Will you leave a message or call back later?

B: When will he come back?

A: He is on his way to our company. Maybe in a few minutes.

B: OK. I will call back. Bye.

A: Bye.

─── Dialogue 2 ───

Can I Help You?

音频 8 - 4

C: Good morning. This is the sale department. Can I help you?

B: Can I speak to Mrs. Wang，please?

C: Yes，I am.

B: Good morning. Mrs. Wang. I'm calling because we will have a meeting at ten o'clock tomorrow in the conference room.

C: Could you repeat the time of the meeting? I can't hear clearly.

B: Yes. Ten o'clock tomorrow morning.

C: What is the objective of tomorrow meeting，please?

B: The topic is about how to increase the dropping sales in Asian markets.

C: OK，I see that. I will arrive on time. Thanks for calling.

B: You are welcome. Bye.

======== **Dialogue 3** ========

Ask for a Leave

音频 8-5

A: Hello!

B: Hello! Good morning. Who is that speaking?

A: It's Jane. I'm so sorry that I made such an early phone call.

B: It's nothing. Who do you wish to talk to?

A: Is Sue James in?

B: Sue! Jane wants you on the phone.

A: Hello! Is Sue there?

C: Yes, speaking.

A: Oh, sorry, I'm afraid I won't attend the meeting this morning. Last night I had a sore throat.

C: Do you have a temperature? Have you taken it?

A: No, haven't yet.

C: Don't worry about the meeting. You'd better go to see a doctor. I wish you will soon be well.

A: Thank you, Sue. Bye.

C: Bye.

Unit 9 Fashion Etiquette

=== Objectives ===

In this unit, the students are required to grasp the following contents.

1. Learning to talk something about fashion etiquette with some given useful words and phrases of this unit freely.

2. Learning to talk something about fashion etiquette with some given useful sentences of this unit freely.

3. Reading a passage about fashion etiquette and then paraphrasing it.

4. Listening and having a role play about fashion etiquette.

······ Part I Preparing ······

 Work individually: What kind of dress do you usually like to wear?

In your dress, you like to wear...	Often	Sometimes	Never
casual clothes			
informal clothes			
lounge suit			
black tie			
white tie			

 Pair work: Compare your answers with a partner.

Why do many people stress dressing on social occasions?

····· **Part II   Performing** ······

Reading

━━━━━ New Words and Phrases ━━━━━

habit ['hæbɪt] *n.* 习惯

garment ['gɑːmənt] *n.* 服装；衣服；外衣

jacket ['dʒækɪt] *n.* 外套；短上衣；夹克

scarf [skɑːf] *n.* 围巾

sleeve [sliːv] *n.* 袖子

jeans [dʒiːnz] *n.* 牛仔裤

boot [buːt] *n.* 靴子，长靴，皮靴

slipper ['slɪpə(r)] *n.* 拖鞋，（室内）便鞋

sandal ['sændl] *n.* 凉鞋，草带鞋

makeup ['meɪkʌp] *n.* 化妆

perfume ['pɜːfjuːm] *n.* 香水；香料；香味；香气

hair [heə(r)] *n.* 发型

bear [beə(r)] *n.* 胡子

formal dress 礼服

clothing mismatch 着装不协调

dress down 因某些场合的需要而穿得朴素些

dress up 打扮；穿上特殊服装；装扮成另一
种样子

business suit 西装；商务套装

business casual 商务休闲服；商务便装

woolen garment 毛呢服装

cotton clothes 棉布服装

silk garment 丝绸服装

chemical fiber garment 化纤服装

fur or leather garment 裘革服装

down garment 羽绒服装

artificial fur and leather garment 人造毛皮服装

men's wear 男式服装

women's wear 女式服装

children's wear 儿童服装

infant's wear 婴儿服装

color collocation 颜色搭配

ironed clothes 熨烫衣服

shave one's face 剃脸上的胡须

body odors 体味

well healed shiny shoes 上过油的闪亮的鞋子

 Group work：Read the following sentences and learn how to use them freely.

1. Do you take care of your clothes? 你是否注意自己的着装?

2. A set of skirt is better. This can show your slim figure.
   穿套裙比较好，这样可以显示出你苗条的身材。

3. Your dressing doesn't match with the job you apply for.
   你的着装与你要应聘的工作不相符。

4. Don't deck yourself up with fine clothes but enrich your mind with profound knowledge.
   不要用华丽的衣服装饰自己，而要用渊博的知识丰富自己。

5. Wear dark colors such as navy blue. 穿深色衣服，例如深蓝色。

6. Iron your clothing to get rid of all wrinkles. 衣服要熨烫，不要有褶皱。

7. Make sure all your zippers are zipped! 确定你的拉链都拉上了!

8. Don't wear a lot of jewelry or large pieces of jewelry. 勿穿戴过多或大型的珠宝首饰。

9. Since I'll have a job interview tomorrow, I want to buy a set of suit and a tie. I don't know what color I should choose. Can you give me some suggestions?

由于明天上午我要去参加一个面试，我想买一套西服和一条领带。我不知道该选什么色的，你能给我一些建议吗？

10. Of course. Generally, in formal situation, men always wear black suit or dark blue suit and also a white shirt.

当然可以。一般在正式场合下，男士都穿黑色或深蓝色的西装，并且常配一件白色衬衣。

11. Red color tie is not fit for interview because it indicates power. How about a lighter color one? 红色领带不适于面试时戴，因为它象征的是权力。浅一点的颜色如何？

12. I think for me and anybody else, a smile and proper clothes can be the most attractive feature, because they can light up the whole person. 我认为我和其他人一样，微笑和适宜的着装是最吸引人的特征，因为它们可以使整个人精神焕发。

13. Then what kind of clothes should I wear? 那我该穿什么样的衣服呢？

14. A set of skirt is better. This can show your slim figure. Please pay attention to the color. Light color is better and don't wear red skirt. And you'd better wear a pair of beautiful shoes. 穿套裙比较好，这样可以显示出你苗条的身材。请注意颜色的选择，浅色的比较好看，一定不要穿红色的套裙。此外，你还要配上一双漂亮的皮鞋。

15. You mean that I should make best use of the advantages and bypass the disadvantages. 你的意思是我应该扬长避短。

16. Make sure your hair is properly groomed. 确定头发梳整齐。

17. Clean your fingernails after nearly trimming them. 修剪完指甲后要清洗干净。

18. Wear shoes that match the color of your outfit. Black is usually the best. 鞋子的颜色和衣服要相称，一般而言黑色最适当。

19. Don't wear shoes that are difficult to walk in. 不要穿不好走路的鞋。

20. Don't wear a lot of perfume. 不要喷洒过重的香水。

21. Don't wear heavy makeup. 不要浓妆艳抹。

22. Style your hair in such a way that does not have to be continually brushed away from your face. 不要把头发梳成需要时时从脸部拨开的发型。

23. Don't have extremely long fingernails. 不要把指甲留得太长。

24. Brush your teeth! 要刷牙！

25. Wear socks that match the color of your shoes. Do not wear white socks! Plain socks (without patterns) are best.

袜子的颜色和鞋子要相称，不要穿白袜子！穿素色（不要有花样）的最好。

26. Don't wear a lot of cologne or heavy aftershave.

古龙水或须后水不要抹得太浓。

Listening 🎧

═══ Useful Expressions ═══

stress dressing 强调着装

elegant dressing 优雅的打扮

convey elegance and connotations 传达优雅
　与内涵

be suited to the occasion 适合场合

different occasions 不同场合

some taboos 有些禁忌

female dressing 女装

keep a sense of 保持一种……的感觉

🎵 Pair work：Listen to the dialogues and fill in the blanks.

═══ Dialogue 1 ═══

Stressing Dressing on Social Occasions（1）

A: Why do many people stress dressing on social _____?

B: To an/ a _____, dressing reflects the civilization of a country. For an individual, elegant dressing can convey elegance and connotations. It also shows one _____ for others.

A: What are the _____ for dressing?

B: First，it should _____ well，be suited to the occasion，also be _____ and elegant.

A: Each person has different _____ concerning dressing.

B: Yes. Dressing should _____ with one's identity，_____，character and different occasions.

A: Dressing is really a science.

B: Indeed it is.

音频 9－1

═══ Dialogue 2 ═══

Stressing Dressing on Social Occasions（2）

A: Can you tell me some taboos _____ female dressing?

B: Sure. My _____ to women，especially for the mainland，is that "you'd better keep a sense of _____（保持一种端庄的感觉）."

A: That is to say，one needn't dress up to the nines or dress to the _____.

B: I mean _____ but not rough，exquisite but not complicated（朴素而不粗糙，精致而不复杂）.

音频 9－2

A: And dressing should _____ the occasions. For example，_____ a wedding，one's dressing should not be more _____ and eye-catching than the bride.

B: For the same reason，attending a funeral，one should not _____ powder herself or wear jewelry.

A: Yes，you are right.

.... Part III　Practicing ....

Reading

================ New Words and Phrases ================

fabric ['fæbrɪk] *n.* 织物；布

wardrobe ['wɔːdrəʊb] *n.* 衣柜，衣橱；藏衣室

convey [kən'veɪ] *v.* 表达；传达，传递

remove [rɪ'muːv] *v.* 去除；开除；脱掉

slightly ['slaɪtli] *adv.* 轻微地，轻轻地

texture ['tekstʃə] *n.* 质地

destination [destɪ'neɪʃən] *n.* 目的，目标；目的地，终点

vary ['veəri] *v.* 变化；不同

reflect [rɪ'flekt] *v.* 反射

strict [strɪkt] *adj.* 精确的；绝对的

profound [prə'faʊnd] *adj.* 深厚的；意义深远的；严重的；知识渊博的

discomfort [dɪs'kʌmfət] *n.* 不安；不舒适，不舒服

therapy ['θerəpi] *n.* 治疗，疗法，疗效

dispel [dɪ'spel] *v.* 驱逐；消除

apparent [ə'pærənt] *adj.* 易看见的，可看见的

blazer ['bleɪzə(r)] *n.* 运动上衣

accessory [ək'sesəri] *n.* 附件

a business setting 商业环境

clothing mismatches 服装不匹配

set strict guidelines 严格的规定

office attire 办公室着装

dress accordingly 穿相应的衣服

a business meeting 商务会议

a senior vice president 高级副总裁

personal appearance 个人仪表

dress-down days 便装日

business professional days 商务专业日

business-professional attire days 商务职业装日子

business casual clothes 商务休闲服

jeans，worn，wrinkled polo shirts 牛仔裤，破旧和皱巴巴的马球衬衫

sneakers，scuffed shoes 运动鞋和磨坏的鞋

halter tops 吊带

revealing blouses 暴露的衬衫

a neat pair of pants 一条整洁的裤子

a buttoned shirt 一件带有纽扣的衬衫

Work individually: Read the following passage and then paraphrase.

Business Dress

Being less than perfectly well-dressed in a business setting can result in a feeling of profound discomfort that may well require therapy to dispel. And the sad truth is that "clothing mismatches" on the job can ruin the day of the person who's wearing inappropriate and the people with whom he or she comes in contact.

When should you dress up or dress down?

Offices vary when it comes to dress codes. Some businesses have very high standards for their employees and set strict guidelines for office attire, while others maintain a more relaxed attitude. However, it is always important to remember that no matter what your company's attitude is regarding what you wear, you are working in a business environment and you should dress accordingly. Certain items may be more appropriate for evening wear than for a business meeting, just as shorts and a T-shirt are better suited for the beach than for an office environment. Your attire should reflect both your environment and your position. A senior vice president has a different image to maintain than that of a secretary or sales assistant. Like it or not, you will be judged by your personal appearance.

This is never more apparent than on "dress-down days", when what you wear can say more about you than any business suit ever could. In fact, people will pay more attention to what you wear on dress-down days than on business professional days. Thus, when dressing in business casual clothes, try to put some flair into your wardrobe choices, recognize that the "real" definition of business casual is to dress just one notch down from what you would normally wear on business professional attire days. Avoid jeans, worn, wrinkled polo shirts, sneakers, scuffed shoes, halter tops, and revealing blouses. For men, try wearing a neat pair of pants and a buttoned shirt with long or short sleeves that has more color or texture in the fabric. For women, wear skirts or tailored pants with blouses, blazers, and accessories that mean business yet convey a more casual look than your standard business attire.

Remember, there are boundaries between your career and your social life. You should dress one way for play and another way when you mean business. Always ask yourself where you're going and how other people will be dressed when you get there. Is the final destination the opera, the beach, or the office? Dress accordingly and you will discover the truth in the axiom that clothes make the man and the woman. When in doubt, always err on the side of dressings lightly more conservatively than the situation demands. Remember, you can always remove a jacket, but you can't put one on if you didn't think to take it with you.

Speaking

======= New Words and Phrases =======

delicate ['delɪkət] *adj.* 微妙的；熟练的；纤
　弱的
vacuum cleaner 真空吸尘器
a pink wig 粉色假发

famous brand 知名品牌
look cute 看起来很可爱
Spice Girls 辣妹组合

Pair work：Listen to the dialogues and have a role play.

====== Dialogue 1 ======

音频 9 - 3

With a Customer

Seller: What can I do for you?

Customer: I want to buy a present for my wife.

Seller: What kind of present does your wife like?

Customer: Maybe something useful and delicate.

Seller: Useful as brooms, delicate as flowers?

Customer: Maybe.

Seller: What about this special designed vacuum cleaner? Look, it is designed for customers with high taste. Your wife will love it, and you will also benefit from this, because when your wife loves working with this, you will have the time to watch football games.

Customer: Deal!

====== Dialogue 2 ======

音频 9 - 4

Which Skirt is Better?

S: What are you going to wear to the dance, Angela?

A: I don't know. How about this red dress?

S: A long dress for a dance? No, I don't think so. How about that black skirt with a yellow blouse? You look great in yellow.

A: No, I always wear this blouse. I have an idea. I am going to wear an orange skirt, a green t-shirt and maybe a pink wig.

Dialogue 3

Buying a Coat

音频 9 - 5

A: May I help you?

B: Yes, please. I want to buy a coat for myself.

A: The coats are over there. This way, please.

B: The black coat looks good. Can I try it on?

A: OK.

B: Oh, it is too small for me! Do you have a larger one?

A: Of course. Here you are.

B: How much is this coat?

A: It is ￥200，this is foreign famous brand.

B: I can't afford your price. Well，make me an offer. The highest I would be willing to buy is ￥100.

A: The lowest I would be willing to sell is ￥150.

B: It's still too much. Can't you make it any cheaper than that?

A: Sorry, this is our lowest price. We can't go any lower.

B: Are you sure?

A: Yes, I'm sure. You won't get it cheaper anywhere in this city.

B: OK. Can I pay by card?

A: Cash or card is fine.

B: I'll pay in cash.

A: It's ￥150 in all.

B: OK. Here is the money.

A: You have given me ￥200，and here is your change of ￥50. Please check it. Would you like a receipt?

B: Yes, of course.

A: Here is your receipt.

B: Thank you very much.

A: You're welcome. Please come again.

Dialogue 4

Buying Clothes

音频 9 - 6

M: Oh, Gucci, the clothes here are expensive! No wonder there are only a few people in here.

G: Beauty costs, friend. Oh, look at this pink skirt, how cute!

M: Believe it or not, they look cute, but not very practical.

G: Come on, Mark. Don't talk like my Mom.

M: When you buy clothes, you must consider the material, quality and price.

G: But fashion changes!

M: Make sure the clothes can be worn for various occasions.

G: All right, Mark. Hey, look, I'm sure this is the same skirt that Spice Girls wear.

M: Definitely! Oh, I love Spice Girls! I'll get this skirt!

Unit 10 Picking Up Etiquette

━━━━ Objectives ━━━━

In this unit, the students are required to grasp the following contents.

1. Learning to talk something about picking up etiquette with some given useful words and phrases of this unit freely.
2. Learning to talk something about picking up etiquette with some given useful sentences of this unit freely.
3. Reading a passage about picking up etiquette and then paraphrasing it.
4. Listening and having a role play about picking up etiquette.

 **Part I Preparing**

 Work individually: What do you like to do when you waiting for airplane?

In the airport, you like...	Often	Sometimes	Never
to sleep			
to play cell phone			
to check the luggage			
to do exercise			
to work			
to eat something			

 Pair work: Compare your answers with a partner.

What do you usually do when you are on the airplane?

······ Part II   Performing ······

Reading

========= New Words and Phrases =========

accommodate [əˈkɒmədeɪt] v. 向……提供住
    处，提供住宿；使适应，使符合一致（to）

competitive [kəmˈpetɪtɪv] adj. 竞争的，比
    赛的

supplier [səˈplaɪə(r)] n. 供应商

appreciate [əˈpriːʃɪeɪt] v. 欣赏，感激，赏识

exhibition [eksɪˈbɪʃən] n. 展示，展览

banquet [ˈbæŋkwɪt] n. 宴会，筵席

manufacture [ˌmænjuˈfæktʃə(r)] vt. 加工；
    n. 制造

limo [ˈlɪmə] n. 豪华轿车

uneventful [ˌʌnɪˈventfl] adj. 平静的；平凡
    的；无特别事件的；平安无事的

unexpectedly [ˌʌnɪkˈspektɪdli] adv. 突然；
    竟；居然；未料到地；意外地

turbulence [ˈtəːbjələns] n. （飞机的）颠簸；
    动荡；骚动；骚乱

appointment [əˈpɔɪntmənt] n. 任命；约会；
    职务；职位

confirm [kənˈfəːm] v. 证实；批准；确认

sight [saɪt] n. 景象；看见；视力；视野；
    景点

be delighted to 很高兴做……

in charge of 对……负责

tie up 无法抽身

be eager to 想要做……

not at all 当然不会；一点也不

pick sb. up 接某人

feel free to do 随意做……

informal dinner 便饭

show sb. around 带某人逛街

trans-Pacific routes 横跨太平洋航线

make sb. comfortable 使某人宾至如归

hear... for a long time 久仰……大名

international passenger 国际旅客

domestic passenger 国内旅客

connecting passenger 转机旅客

transit passenger 过境旅客

emigration control 出境检查

waiting room 休息室

exchange and tax payment 兑换及付税

customs personnel 海关人员

customs inspection counter 海关检查柜台

baggage claim area 行李认领区

immigration control 入境检查

plant quarantine 植物检疫

animal quarantine 动物检疫

arrival lobby 入境旅客休息室

Group work：Read the following sentences and learn how to use them freely.

1. How was your flight? Was it comfortable? 你坐的班机怎么样？还舒服吗？

2. It was quite good. But it was awfully long. 班机很好，就是时间太长了。

3. Did you have a good flight? 你旅途愉快吗?

4. Not really, I'm afraid. We were delayed taking off, and we encountered a lot of bad weather. 恐怕不太好,我们起飞延误了,还遭遇了恶劣的天气。

5. How was your flight? 你的航班怎样?

6. Did you get any sleep on the plane? 你在飞机上睡觉了吗?

7. I've made a reservation at the hotel you used last time. 我已预订了你上次住过的旅馆。

8. We've booked a Western-style room for you. 我们已为你订了一间西式的房间。

9. There's a shuttle bus we can use. 我们可搭乘机场班车。

10. I've brought my car, so I can drive you to your hotel. 我开车来的,所以我开车送你到旅馆。

11. How is your room? 你的房间怎样?

12. Did you sleep well last night? 你昨晚睡得好吗?

13. The tour will take about an hour and a half. We ought to be back here by 3:00. 参观大概要一个半小时,我们应该会在 3 点钟以前回到这里。

14. Our new product line has been very successful. We've expanded the factory twice this year already. 我们新的生产线非常成功,我们今年已把工厂扩展了两倍。

15. Is there anything I can explain fully? 有什么事情要我详细说明的吗?

16. Do you know where the baggage claim area is? 您知道行李认领处在哪儿吗?

17. There's no arrangement tomorrow. Have a good rest and recover from the jet lag. 明天没有安排,请好好休息,倒倒时差。

Listening

━━ **Useful Expressions** ━━

best-selling 畅销　　　　　　　　after-sales 售后

Research and Development Department 研发部　　market products 销售产品

Sunshine Import & Export Co. Ltd 阳光进出口有限公司

chemical product 化学制品　　　　Dispatch Department 派遣部门,运输部门

Rongalite C 98 PCT in lumps 98%雕白块(块状)

after-sales department 售后服务部门

Pair work： Listen to the dialogues and fill in the blanks.

═══ Dialogue 1 ═══

Introducing the Company

Miss Wang and Miss Li are introducing the company to Mr. Johns.

W: Here is our company，Sunshine Import & Export Co. Ltd.

J: Yes，I've _____ the company for a long time.

W: Well，we have been in this line for a long time. And we are one of the most _____ suppliers of this line. We have nearly 280 _____ and sales of ＄9,806 million. We _____ fine chemicals，e. g. Rongalite C 98 PCT in lumps. Our products are _____ in Britain，America，Japan，Italy and South East Asia and well appreciated by their purchasers.

L: Yes，and we always take customers first.

J: Great. Do you have any new _____?

W: Yes，it is researched by our Research and Development Department. I think it will be the _____ line.

J: Wonderful. Can I have a look at these new products?

W: Of course，Miss Li will show you _____ the different departments of our company，and then we will visit the products.

═══ Dialogue 2 ═══

Introducing the Department

L: Follow me，please，Mr. Johns. This is our Marketing Department.

J: Looks great.

L: Yes. Marketing Department _____ advertises and markets products. And this way，this is our Research and Development Department.

J: I've heard a new _____ of chemical product has been _____ by this department.

L: Yes，this department is very _____ for the company. It is called "heart" of the company.

J: Do you have a Dispatch Department?

L: Of course，please turn right，and this is our Dispatch Department，which is _____ to send goods to customers. And we have a great _____ department.

J: It means whatever _____ problems we have after sales，we can get help from this department.

L: Yes，we always take customers as our Gods. Our after-sales _____ is perfect.

······ Part III Practicing ······

Reading

New Words and Phrases

preference ['prefrəns] *n.* 偏爱；优先权；偏爱的事物

refresh [rɪ'freʃ] *v.* 使恢复，使振作

a summer vacation 暑假

depend on 依赖；相信

refresh oneself 提神；解乏

see the countryside 看看农村

on a grass covered path 在草覆盖的小路上

detach from 使从……分离（或分开、脱离、拆开）

closer to the nature 更加亲近自然

becoming available 成为可用的

 Work individually：Read the following passage and then paraphrase.

There are many ways of traveling such as by plane, by train, by ship, by bus. And people can choose any of ways of traveling they like. To me, the best way of traveling on a summer vacation is to go on foot.

My preference depends on the purpose of the travel. On a summer vacation I travel to refresh myself and to see the countryside. When I use my feet and walk on a grass covered path along a river or among the hills, I feel detached from the noise of the city and closer to the nature. And when I travel on foot I get more freedom. I can plan my own schedule. I can choose my own route. I can stop where I like. And I can see things and people that I might miss if I travel on a train or on a bus.

When faster and more convenient ways for travel are becoming available, I still favor using my own feet. I get much pleasure from it. People travel by plane, by train, by ship, by bus. To me, the best way of traveling on a summer vacation is to go on foot.

Speaking

New Words and Phrases

regards [rɪ'gɑːdz] *n.* 问候

send his regards to you 代他向您致意

a really nice guy 一个大好人

free tour guide 免费的导游

product exhibition room 产品陈列室

visit the products 参观产品

latest products 最新产品

in a word 总之；一句话；总而言之；简言之

excellent qualities 优秀品质
reasonable prices 合理的价格
5-year warranty 5 年保修
the best service conditions 最佳服务条件

rely on 依赖，依靠
details of the contract 合同的细节
Export Commodities Fair 出口商品交易会
on display 展出

 Pair work：Listen to the dialogues and have a role play.

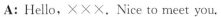
Dialogue 1

At the Airport

A: Hello，×××. Nice to meet you.

B: Nice to meet you，too.

A: Welcome to Guilin. ××× lets me send his regards to you.

B: Oh，he's a really nice guy.

A: Yes，he is. Is it your first time to Guilin?

B: Yes，I've heard a lot about it.

A: Really? Great. Then I can take you on a city tour some time. Free tour guide.

B: Thank you.

音频 10 - 3

Dialogue 2

In a Hotel

A: Is the room Ok?

B: Yes，very good.

A: Great. If you have any need，just feel free to ask.

B: OK. Thank you.

A: Any drink，coffee or water?

B: Coffee is fine.

音频 10 - 4

Dialogue 3

Introducing the Products

Miss Wang and Miss Li are introducing the products to Mr. Johns.

W: Mr. Johns，now let me show you around our product exhibition room.

J: I can hardly wait to visit the products.

L: This way，please.

W: OK，we are in the product exhibition room. Our latest products are exhibited here.

L: Yes，in a word，our products have the excellent qualities and reasonable prices. We have 5-year warranty and the best service conditions. You can rely on us.

音频 10 - 5

J: I am really interested in Type 1 &.2. Would it be possible for me to have a closer look at your samples?

W: Of course, please.

J: Now I can't wait to consult the details of the contract.

 Dialogue 4

音频 10 - 6

At the Export Commodities Fair

Miss Wang, the sales manager, is taking Mr. Johns to visit the Export Commodities Fair.

W: Mr. Johns, this way, please. The fair has been held once a year since 1990. Many visitors come to the Fair every year. And the number of visitors is increased every year. This year the number is expected to be over 10 000.

J: I am excited to be here. How crowded with the people!

W: Yes. Be careful. The Fair has become very important in our foreign trade. There are about 20 000 new products on display. Many Chinese foreign trade companies come here and do both import and export business here.

J: I suppose these products at the exhibition fair must be quite new in design. I am interested in looking around.

W: OK, let's go.

Unit 11 Conference Etiquette

In this unit, the students are required to grasp the following contents.

1. Learning to talk something about conference etiquette with some given useful words and phrases of this unit freely.
2. Learning to talk something about conference etiquette with some given useful sentences of this unit freely.
3. Reading a passage about conference etiquette and then paraphrasing it.
4. Listening and having a role play about conference etiquette.

 Part I   Preparing

 Work individually: What do you like to do when having a conference?

On conference, you like...	Often	Sometimes	Never
to play some games in your cell phone			
to chat with others			
to listen carefully and record			
to do some work			
to read books			
to sleep			

 Pair work: Compare your answers with a partner.

If you have different ideas on a conference, what do you do?

········· **Part II   Performing** ·······

Reading

━━━━━ New Words and Phrases ━━━━━

meeting [ˈmiːtɪŋ] *n.* 会议

conference [ˈkɒnfərəns] *n.* 会议

convention [kənˈvenʃn] *n.* 会议，年会，例会

exposition [ˌekspəˈzɪʃn] *n.* 博览会

workshop [ˈwəːkʃɒp] *n.* 研讨会

forum [ˈfɔːrəm] *n.* 论坛

seminar [ˈsemɪnɑː(r)] *n.* 研究会

panel [ˈpænl] *n.* 座谈小组

debate [dɪˈbeɪt] *n.* 辩论会

session [ˈseʃn] *n.* 会议

clarification [ˌklærəfɪˈkeɪʃn] *n.* 澄清

comment [ˈkɒment] *n.* 评论

consensus [kənˈsensəs] *n.* 共识

reject [rɪˈdʒekt] *v.* 拒绝，驳回

resolution [ˌrezəˈluːʃn] *n.* 决议

trade show 行业展览会，博览会

corporate meeting 公司会议

association meeting 社团会议，协会会议

general session 全体大会

at the moment 此刻

rural market 农村市场

take place 发生

opening sitting 开幕会

final sitting 闭幕会

formal sitting 隆重开会

to make a speech/to deliver a speech 做报告

advisory opinion 顾问意见

declare close 宣布结束

annual convention 年会，年度大会

new product introduction 新产品发布会

teleconferencing 电话会议

opening welcome reception 欢迎招待会

lecture-formatted meeting 演讲式会议

slide presentation 幻灯演示

host country 东道国

in the name of 以……的名义

signing ceremony 签字仪式

meeting facility 会议设施

meeting planner 会议筹谋人

first draft 草案初稿

operative part 生效部分

factual report 事实报告

summary record 摘要纪录

draft resolution 决议草案，提案

raise an objection 提出异议

move an amendment 提出修正案

substantive motion 实质性的动议

 Group work：Read the following sentences and learn how to use them freely.

1. Let me introduce you to Mr. Li, general manager of our company.

   让我介绍你认识，这是我们的总经理李先生。

2. It's an honor to meet you. 很荣幸认识你。

3. Nice to meet you. I've heard a lot about you. 很高兴认识你，久仰大名。

4. Now that everyone is here，let's get down to business.

现在大家都在这里，让我们着手议正事。

5. We are going to discuss three problems this morning. 今天上午我们要讨论三个问题。

6. Shall we move on to the next item on the agenda? 我们可以进入下一项议程了吗？

7. First，I'd like Mr. Hunter to introduce the situation briefly.

首先，我想请亨特先生简略介绍一下有关情况。

8. Come back to the main point. 回到正题上。

9. I think we are getting side-tracked. 我认为我们跑题了。

10. Shall we get back to the main point? 我们可以回到正题上吗？

11. I'm afraid we're getting a bit off the point. 我恐怕我们有点跑题了。

12. I see your point, but could we stick to the main problem?

我明白你的意思，但我们应该坚持谈论主要问题，对吧？

13. Declare results. 宣布结果。

14. The meeting is adjourned. 会议暂停。

15. Let me take a minute to sum up the main points of this discussion.

请允许我概括本次讨论要点。

16. If nobody wants to add anything，we can draw the meeting to a close.

如果没有人要补充，我们可以闭会了。

Listening

Useful Expressions

first of all 首先　　　　　　　　Southwest Area Sales Vice President 西南地区销售副总裁

look forward to 期望　　　　　　national sales director 全国销售总监

Far East sales force 远东销售力　　market areas 市场领域

go over the report 再看一遍报告，修改一下报告　the last meeting 最近一次会议

sales reporting system 销售报告系统　move on to 移动到……

a brainstorming session 头脑风暴会议

concerning after sales customer support improvements 关于售后客户支持的改进

 Pair work：Listen to the dialogues and fill in the blanks.

Dialogue 1

Business Meetings Introduction

音频 11-1

Meeting Chairman: If we are all here，let's get _____. First of all，I'd like you to please _____ me in welcoming Jack Peterson，our Southwest Area Sales Vice President.

Jack Peterson: Thank you for having me；I'm looking _____ to today's meeting.

Meeting Chairman: I'd also like to _____ Margaret Simmons who recently joined our team.

Margaret Simmons: May I also introduce my assistant，Bob Hamp?

Meeting Chairman: Welcome Bob. I'm _____ our national sales director，Anne Trusting，can't be _____ us today. She is in Kobe at the _____ _____ , developing our Far East sales force.

═══ **Dialogue 2** ═══

Reviewing Past Business

音频 11-2

Meeting Chairman: Let's get _____ . We're here today to _____ ways of _____ sales in _____ market areas. First，let's go over the report from the last meeting which was _____ on June 24th. Right，Tom，over to you.

Tom Robbins: Thank you，Mark. Let me just summarize the main _____ of the last meeting. We began the meeting by approving the changes in our sales reporting system discussed on May 30th. After briefly revising the changes that will take _____ , we moved on to a brainstorming session concerning after sales customer support improvements. You'll find a copy of the main ideas developed and discussed in these _____ _____ in the photocopies in _____ of you. The meeting was _____ _____ closed at 11：30.

······· **Part III   Practicing** ·······

Reading

═══ New Words and Phrases ═══

propose [prə'pəʊz] *v.* 提议，建议；打算
proposal [prə'pəʊzl] *n.* 建议
stand [stænd] *n.* 立场，主张
handout ['hændaʊt] *n.* 讲义；救济品，施舍物；印刷品

in attendance 出席；当值
a copy of the agenda 一份会议议程
have a mountain of work to do 有一大堆工作要做
run through 贯穿；跑着穿过……

budget review 预算审查	的细节
come up with 想出；提出；追赶上	the final review handout 最后的修改讲义
a final review 最后的审查	objections or corrections 反对或修正
a few polishing details left 剩下的一些需完善	

 Work individually：Read the following passage and then paraphrase.

M: I call this meeting to order. Thank you all in attendance today. I know it's a busy day for you all. We have a lot of materials to cover today. Did everyone get an agenda?

F: I need a copy of the agenda. Also，may I suggest something? I know we have many points to review today，but would it be possible to limit our meeting time to finish before four o'clock? Many of us still have a mountain of work to do before the day's end.

M: We should be able to finish everything up before then. Let's run through the major points first，and see where we're at. The first matter of business is to approve the minutes of our last meeting.

F: I propose we accept the minutes.

M: Good. Do I have a second?

F: One second.

M: Motion is carried. Now，next on our agenda is our budget review. Margaret，can you please fill us in on where the budget review stands?

F: I gave everyone a copy of the manual last week. We've had the review board going over everything，and they have come up with a final review. Here's a copy for everyone，and if you have any question，you can talk to me after the meeting. Basically，the budget review has been completed，maybe with a few polishing details left.

M: What kind of action is required?

F: Please take a look at the final review handout. If there're any objections or corrections，let me know. Next week，we can cast the final approval.

Speaking

━━━━━ New Words and Phrases ━━━━━

rural ['rʊərəl] *adj.* 乡下的，农村的
appointment [ə'pɒɪntmənt] *n.* 任命
speaker ['spiːkə(r)] *n.* 扬声器
procedure [prə'siːdʒə(r)] *n.* 程序
support [sə'pɔːt] *vt.* 赞成

oppose [ə'pəʊz] *v.* 反对
amend [ə'mend] *v.* 修正
record ['rekɒd] *n.* 记录
report [rɪ'pɒːt] *n.* 报告
rural sales 农村销售

sales districts 销售区域

go round 转动；到处走动；参观；走访

in one's opinion 在……看来

urban customers 城市的客户

return to 返回到……；重新恢复

rural base 农村基地

develop an advertising campaign 开发一项广
　　告活动

particular needs 特殊需求

information reporting 信息报告

sales staff 销售人员

database information 数据库信息

as you can see 正如你所看到的；如你所见

break up into groups 分成不同的小组

rules of procedure 议事规则

item on the agenda 议程项目

other business 其他事项

place... on the agenda 把……列入议程

working paper 工作文件

specific data 特定数据；具体数据

mining procedures 开采程序

the experienced and proficient secretary 有经
　　验的、熟练的秘书

a junior secretary 初级秘书

make a note of 把……记下来

the general manager 总经理

Pair work：Listen to the dialogues and have a role play.

音频 11 - 3

===== **Dialogue 1** =====

Conference Discussing Items

Jack Peterson: Before I begin the report，I'd like to get some ideas from you all. How do you feel about rural sales in your sales districts? I suggest we go round the table first to get all of your input.

John Ruting: In my opinion，we have been focusing too much on urban customers and their needs. The way I see things，we need to return to our rural base by developing an advertising campaign to focus on their particular needs.

Alice Linnes: I'm afraid I can't agree with you. I think rural customers want to feel as important as our customers living in cities. I suggest we give our rural sales team more help with advanced customer information reporting.

Donald Peters: Excuse me，I didn't catch that. Could you repeat that，please?

Alice Linnes: I just stated that we need to give our rural sales team better customer information reporting.

John Ruting: I don't quite follow you. What exactly do you mean?

Alice Linnes: Well，we provide our city sales staff with database information on all of our larger clients. We should be providing the same sort of knowledge on our rural customers to our sales staff there.

Jack Peterson: Would you like to add anything，Jennifer?

Jennifer Miles: I must admit I never thought about rural sales that way before. I have to agree with Alice.

Jack Peterson: Well, let me begin with this Power Point presentation (Jack presents his report).

Jack Peterson: As you can see, we are developing new methods to reach out to our rural customers.

John Ruting: I suggest we break up into groups and discuss the ideas we've seen presented.

=== Dialogue 2 ===

Changing Time for the Meeting

音频 11-4

Meeting Chairman: Unfortunately, we're running short of time. We'll have to leave that to another time.

Jack Peterson: Before we close, let me just summarize the main points:

- Rural customers need special help to feel more valued.
- Our sales teams need more accurate information on our customers.
- A survey will be completed to collect data on spending habits in these areas.
- The results of this survey will be delivered to our sales teams.
- We are considering specific data mining procedures to help deepen our understanding.

Meeting Chairman: Thank you very much, Jack. Right, it looks as though we've covered the main items. Is there any other business?

Donald Peters: Can we fix the next meeting, please?

Meeting Chairman: Good idea, Donald. How does Friday in two weeks time sound to everyone? Let's meet at the same time, 9 o'clock. Is that Ok for everyone? Excellent. I'd like to thank Jack for coming to our meeting today. The meeting is closed.

=== Dialogue 3 ===

Preparing for the Meeting

音频 11-5

Ms Wang, the experienced and proficient secretary, is asking Miss Zhou, a junior secretary, whether she has prepared well for the meeting.

(A: Ms Wang; B: Miss Zhou)

A: Is the room ready for the meeting, Miss Zhou?

B: Yes, I've put the Minute Book and some paper copies of the agenda on the table. And paper and pencils have been laid by their name-cards on the conference table for each attendant.

A: Thank you. How about the microphone and speakers?

B: I also have got them ready for the meeting.

A: Good. I've come to tell you that you'll have to take the minutes this afternoon.

B: Should I write down every word that everyone says?

A: No, you needn't. That's very difficult and hardly ever necessary. You just make a note of the topics that are discussed and the result of the discussion.

B: And should I type out the minutes from the notes?

A: Yes, of course.

音频 11 - 6

━━ Dialogue 4 ━━

About Meeting Schedule

A: Mr. Black, I come to remind you of a meeting scheduled from ten o'clock this morning.

B: Oh, that's right. And the general manager asked me to report on the company's sales for last year at the meeting.

A: By the way, the meeting will be held in your office, not in the conference room.

B: OK, thank you very much.

A: Not at all. That's what I should do.

Unit 12 Dining Etiquette

■ Objectives ■

In this unit, the students are required to grasp the following contents.

1. Learning to talk something about dining etiquette with some given useful words and phrases of this unit freely.

2. Learning to talk something about dining etiquette with some given useful sentences of this unit freely.

3. Reading a passage about dining etiquette of western dinner party and then paraphrasing it.

4. Listening and having a role play about dining etiquette.

······· **Part I   Preparing** ·······

 Work individually: How often do you like to enjoy these cuisines?

In these cuisines, you like...	Often	Sometimes	Never
Chinese cuisine			
French cuisine			
Italian cuisine			
Mexico cuisine			
American cuisine			
Japanese cuisine			

 Pair work: Compare your answers with a partner.

In my spare time, I often cook at home. How about you?

⋯⋯ Part II　Performing ⋯⋯

Reading

━━━ New Words and Phrases ━━━

menu ['menjuː] *n.* 菜单

order [ɒ'ːdə(r)] *v.* 点餐

pudding ['pudɪŋ] *n.* 布丁

harmful ['hɑːmfl] *adj.* 有害的

delicious [dɪ'lɪʃəs] *adj.* 美味的

drink [drɪŋk] *n.* 饮料

beer [bɪə(r)] *n.* 啤酒

wine [waɪn] *n.* 葡萄酒

distillate ['dɪstɪleɪt] *n.* 馏分油；馏出物，馏
　出液，蒸馏液

spirits ['spɪrɪts] *n.* 白酒

champagne [ʃæm'peɪn] *n.* 香槟酒

cocktail ['kɒkteɪl] *n.* 鸡尾酒

vodka ['vɒdkə] *n.* 伏特加

whisky ['wɪskɪ] *n.* 威士忌

brandy ['brændi] *n.* 白兰地

cognac ['kɒnjæk] *n.* 法国白兰地

gin [dʒɪn] *n.* 杜松子酒

martini [mɑː'tiːni] *n.* 马提尼酒

condiment ['kɒndɪmənt] *n.* 调味品

hospitality [ˌhɒspɪ'tæləti] *n.* 好客，热情款待

tasty ['teɪsti] *adj.* 可口的，好吃的

crispy ['krɪspi] *adj.* 卷曲的，松脆的

medium ['miːdɪəm] *adj.* 五分熟的

rare [reə(r)] *adj.* 三分熟的

leftover ['leftəʊvə] *n.* 吃剩的食物

pancake ['pænkeɪk] *n.* 薄煎饼

alcohol concentration 酒精浓度

well done 全熟

serving order 上菜顺序

western tableware 西方餐具

main course 主菜

mashed potatoes 马铃薯泥

black coffee 纯咖啡

white coffee 牛奶咖啡

black tea 红茶

rice wine 米酒

mineral water 矿泉水

orange juice 橘汁

soup spoon 汤匙

eggs sunny side up 煎一面的鸡蛋

cole slaw 卷心菜丝

hit the spot 合口味

eat out 外面吃

in order to 为了

balanced diet 平衡饮食

🐾 **Group work**：Read the following sentences and learn how to use them freely.

1. I'd have beefsteak. 我要牛排。

2. Would you like the steak well done or rare?
　您喜欢牛排煎得透一点，还是略生一点？

3. What would you like for dessert? 想要什么甜点呢?

4. I'll have the fillet of beef with cauliflower. 我要牛肉片配花椰菜。

5. What dressing would you like on the salad? 您的色拉要加什么调料?

6. Would you like to have an assorted fresh fruit in season?
   您想来一个时令新鲜水果拼盘吗?

7. Would you like ketchup or mustard? 你喜欢番茄酱还是芥末?

8. Is there anything else you need? 还要别的吗?

9. How would you like us to cook your eggs? 您的鸡蛋要我们怎么做?

10. We can serve pancakes very quickly. 我们可以很快供应薄饼。

Listening 🎧

===== **Useful Expressions** =====

a bowl of rice 一碗米饭　　　　　　around corner 墙角

make dinner 做晚餐　　　　　　　　biology teacher 生物老师;生物教师

on the menu 在菜单上

Pair work:Listen to the dialogues and fill in the blanks.

===== Dialogue 1 =====

Ordering (1)

音频 12‑1

W: Sir,what can I do _____ you?

C: I'd like to have a table _____ corner,quiet.

W: OK,please _____ me.

C: May I have the _____ ?

W: Sure,here you are.(After a few minutes)

C: I'd like to _____ a _____ of wine,oh; I nearly _____ I'll drive. Please just a _____ of juice, a bowl of rice and a fish.

W: Is this all?

C: Well,the biscuit on the menu _____ very nice,so a piece of this one.

W: Please wait a _____ .

Dialogue 2

Ordering（2）

音频 12 - 2

Ann: Mom，what do we _____ for dinner?

Mom: How _____ fish, fruit salad, and bread?

Dad: I just want to eat _____. I don't think we have _____ time to make dinner.

Bob: Mom, our biology teacher told me we shouldn't eat _____ fruit, that's _____ to the body. And Dad, most of the restaurants put too much oil to the meal in _____ ____ to make the meals taste _____; actually it's bad for our _____.

Ann: I agree with Bob. Let's eat salad and bread and some egg, that's the _____ diet.

Mom: Well done. I think you are great. Mom and Dad really should learn something new.

········ **Part III　Practicing** ········

Reading

━━━ New Words and Phrases ━━━

napkin ['næpkɪn] *n.* 餐巾，餐巾纸	for the first time 首次；第一次
knife [naɪf] *n.* 刀	table manners 餐桌礼仪
fork [fɔːk] *n.* 叉子	Western culture 西方文化
starter ['stɑːtə(r)] *n.* 开胃菜	damp cloth 湿布；湿巾
dessert [dɪ'zɜːt] *n.* 饭后甜点	a bowl of soup 一碗汤
a formal Western dinner party 正式的西式宴会	main course 主菜；大菜

 Work individually: Read the following passage and then paraphrase.

People who go to a formal Western dinner party for the first time may be surprised by table manners in Western culture. Knowing them will help you make a good impression. Having good table manners means knowing, for example, how to use knives and forks, when to drink a toast and how to behave at the table. Beside your napkin you will find a small bread roll and three glasses—one for white wine, one for red wine, and one for water. There are two pairs of knives and forks on the table, forks on the left and knives on the right of the plate. When you see two spoons, the big one is for the soup and the small one is for the dessert. The knife and the fork that are closest to your plate are a little bit bigger than the ones beside them. When you sit down at the table, you can take your napkin, unfold it and put it on your lap. In China you sometime get a hot, damp cloth to clean your face and hands, which, however, is the custom in Western countries.

Dinner starts with a small dish, which is often called a starter. Some people pray before they start eating, and other people may keep silent for a moment. Then you can say "Enjoy your meal" to each other and everybody start eating. For the starter, which you eat with the smaller pair, you keep the knife in your right hand and the fork in your left. After the starter you will get a bowl of soup—but only one bowl of soup and never ask for a second serving.

The next dish is the main course. Many Westerners think the chicken breast with its tender white flesh is the best part of the bird. Some people can use their fingers when they are eating chicken or other birds, but never touch beef or other meat in bones. It is polite to finish eating everything on your plate, so don't take more food than you need.

At table, you should try to speak quietly and smile a lot, but do not laugh all the time. Most Westerners like soft drink if they will drive home. Many of them drink white or red wine with the food. When drinking to someone's health, you raise your glasses, but the glasses should not touch. The custom of toasting in some parts of China is to finish the drink at once, but Westerners usually take only a sip. For drinking during a dinner, the best advice is never to drink too much.

Table manners change over time. They follow the fashion of the day. Beside, table manners are only important at formal dinner parties. If you're not sure what to do, you can always follow your hosts. Although good manners always make you look good, you do not need to worry about all these rules while having dinner with your friends or family.

Speaking

New Words and Phrases
---

tempting ['temptɪŋ] *adj.* 诱人的；吸引人的　　　a cup of coffee 一杯咖啡

salad ['sæləd] *n.* 沙拉　　　　　　　　　　　a banana pie 一个香蕉派

pumpkin pies 南瓜馅饼；南瓜饼　　　　　　　a vegetable salad 一份蔬菜沙拉

Pair work: Listen to the dialogues and have a role play.

--- Dialogue 1 ---

Choosing Food（1）

音频 12 - 3

Hostess: Would you like to have some more chicken?

Guest: No, thank you. The chicken is very delicious, but I'm just too full.

Host: But I hope you saved room for dessert. Mary makes very good pumpkin pies.

Guest: That sounds very tempting. But I hope we can wait a little while, if you don't mind.

Host: Of course. How about some coffee or tea now?

Guest: Tea, please. Thanks.

Dialogue 2

Choosing Food（2）

音频 12-4

W: Can I help you?

G: I'd like a fish.

W: What would you like to drink?

G: May I have a cup of coffee?

W: Yes, sir. Would you care for some desserts?

G: Yes, I'd love a banana pie.

W: Anything else, sir?

G: And give me some ice-cream.

W: What flavor would you like?

G: Chocolate, please.

W: OK. I'll be back with your food soon.

Dialogue 3

Western Food

音频 12-5

W: May I help you?

G: Well, this is my first time to try Western food and I really don't know what to have.

W: May I recommend something?

G: Yes, please.

W: Our lobster is good. Would you like to have a try?

G: Yes. And I'd also like to have a vegetable salad.

W: Do you want anything to drink, sir?

G: Beer, please.

W: Wait a moment. I'll be back soon.

Dialogue 4

At a Restaurant

音频 12-6

W: Welcome to our restaurant.

G: Thank you.

W: May I take your order now?

G: Yes, I'll have a beef steak.

W: How would you like your beef steak?

G: Half done.

W: Would you like something to drink?

G: Yes, a cup of coffee.

W: Would you prefer your coffee with sugar or with milk?

G: With milk.

W: Will there be anything else?

G: No, that's all.

Unit 13 Negotiation Etiquette

In this unit, the students are required to grasp the following contents.

1. Learning to talk something about negotiation etiquette with some given useful words and phrases of this unit freely.

2. Learning to talk something about negotiation etiquette with some given useful sentences of this unit freely.

3. Reading a passage about negotiation etiquette and then paraphrasing it.

4. Listening and having a role play about negotiation etiquette.

····· Part I   Preparing ·····

 Work individually: What is the reason you make negotiation?

Why make negotiation, the purpose is...	Often	Sometimes	Never
to gain the benefit			
to satisfy the needs			
to seek interest			
to pursue cooperation			
to seek common points and mutual benefits			
to discuss the conflicts			

 Pair work: Compare your answers with a partner.

In a negotiation, how do you make a compromise?

······ Part II Performing ······

Reading

==== New Words and Phrases ====

customer ['kʌstəmə(r)] n. 顾客，消费者

extract ['ekstrækt] v. 取出，摘录

irrelevant ['ɪreləvənt] adj. 不相关的，不切题的

relevant ['reləvənt] adj. 有关的

sample ['sɑːmpl] n. 样品

wavy ['weɪvi] adj. 波状的，波动的

assemble [ə'sembl] v. 集合，装配

agent ['eɪdʒənt] n. 代理人

compile [kəm'paɪl] v. 编辑，汇编

contract ['kɒntrækt] n. 合同，契约

submit [səb'mɪt] v. 提交，递交

discount ['dɪskaʊnt] n. 折扣

co-worker [ˌkəʊ'wɜːkə] n. 合作者，同事

proportion [prə'pɔːʃn] n. 比例，部分

copy ['kɒpi] n. 副本

concise [kən'saɪs] adj. 简洁的

courteous ['kɜːtɪəs] adj. 有礼貌的

heading ['hedɪŋ] n. 标题

recycle [ˌriː'saɪkl] v. 回收再利用

manual ['mænjuəl] n. 手册，指南

additive ['ædətɪv] n. 添加剂

artificial [ˌɑːtɪ'fɪʃl] adj. 人造的，假的

economy [ɪ'kɒnəmi] n. 经济实惠，节约措施

output ['aʊtpʊt] n. 产量，输出量

range [reɪndʒ] n. 种类

responsibility [rɪspɒnsə'bɪləti] n. 责任，职责

guarantee [ˌɡærən'tiː] v. 保证，担保

slash [slæʃ] v. 大幅削减；挥砍

business card 名片

e-mail 电子邮件

order book 订货簿

lead time 订货至交货的时间

have a significant impact on 对……有重大影响

derive from 追溯，起源

confer with somebody 和某人商谈

assign a definition to... 给……下一个定义

a give-and-take trading process 公平交易的贸易过程

back-and-forth 反反复复

spell out 讲清楚

bargaining strength 谈判中的优势强项，谈判中的长处

be weighted in one's own favor 对某人有利

ideological differences 意识形态的差异

frame of reference 参照系

a country's balance of payments 一个国家的支付平衡

strike a deal 成交

arrive at compromises 达成妥协

hold all the aces 握有王牌

squeeze... out 榨取

take or leave it 或取或舍，悉听尊便

horse trading 讨价还价后达成的交易

concession trading 让步贸易

problem-solving device 解决冲突的方法

back-and-forth communication 反反复复的交流

at a crucial point 在关键时刻

a set of issues 一系列的问题

be cut to 生来就适合于

mental acuity 才智敏锐

allow for 考虑到，顾及；体谅

middle ground 中间立场，中间观点

order form 订购单

come up to expectations 尽如人意

feed back 反馈，反应

long-standing 长期的

 Group work：Read the following sentences and learn how to use them freely.

1. Our position on the issue is very simple. 我们的意见很简单。

2. We can not be sure what you want unless you tell us.
   希望你能告诉我们，要不然我们无法确定你想要什么。

3. We have done a lot. 我们已经取得了不少的进展。

4. We can work out the details next time. 我们可以下次再来解决细节问题。

5. I suggest that we take a break. 我建议我们休息一下。

6. Let's dismiss and return in an hour. 咱们休会，一个小时后再回来。

7. We need a break. 我们需要暂停一下。

8. May I suggest that we continue tomorrow? 我建议明天再继续，好吗？

9. We can postpone our meeting until tomorrow. 我们可以把会议延迟到明天。

10. That will eat up a lot of time. 那会耗费很多时间。

11. We'll come out from this meeting as winners. 这次会谈我们将双赢。

12. I hope this meeting is productive. 我希望这是一次富有成效的会谈。

13. Frankly, we can't agree with your proposal. 坦白地讲，我无法同意您的提案。

14. I wonder if you have found that our specifications meet your requirements. I'm sure the prices we submitted are competitive.
    不知道您认为我们的规格是否符合你的要求？我敢肯定我们的价格是非常有竞争力的。

15. We offer you our best prices, at which we have done a lot of business with other customers.
    我们向你们报最优惠价，按此价我们已与其他客户做了大批生意。

Listening 🎧

 **Useful Expressions**

get the ball rolling 开始；启动；开个头，使开始，使展开

have in mind 想到   research costs 研发成本   slash your costs 大量减低成本

turn over 使翻转   make a profit 盈利   Exec-U-ciser 某种健身器材的商标

take a cut 降低   common ground 共同的信念

🌟 **Pair work**：Listen to the dialogues and fill in the blanks.

━━━━ Dialogue 1 ━━━━

音频 13-1

Talking About Prices

D: I'd like to get the ball _____ by talking about prices.

R: I'd be happy to _____ any questions you may have.

D: Your products are very good. But I'm a little _____ about the prices you're asking.

R: You think we should be asking for more? (Laughs)

D: (Chuckles) That's not _____ what I had in _____. I know your _____ costs are high，but what I'd like is a 25% discount.

R: That seems to be a little high，Mr. Smith. I don't know how we can make a _____ with those numbers.

D: Please，Robert，call me Dan. (Pause) Well，if we promise future business — volume sales — that will slash your _____ for making the Exec -U-ciser，right?

R: Yes，but it's hard to see how you can place such large orders. How could you turn _____ _____ so many? (Pause) We'd need a _____ of future business，not just a promise.

D: We said we wanted 1000 pieces over a six-month period. What if we place orders for twelve months，with a guarantee?

R: If you can guarantee that on paper，I think we can discuss this further.

━━━━ Dialogue 2 ━━━━

音频 13-2

Exercises

R: Even with volume sales，our costs for the Exec -U-ciser won't go _____ much.

D: Just what are you proposing?

R: We can take a _____ on the price. But 25% would slash our _____ margin. We suggest a _____ —10%.

D: That's a big change from 25 to 10 and it is _____ my negotiating _____. (Pause) Any other ideas?

R: I don't think I can _____ it right now. Why don't we talk _____ tomorrow?

D: Sure. I must talk to my _____ anyway. I hope we can find some _____ ground on this.

······· **Part III Practicing** ·······

Reading

━━━━ **New Words and Phrases** ━━━━

executive [ɪɡˈzekjətɪv] *n.* 总经理；行政部门

investment [ɪnˈvestmənt] *n.* 投资，投资额

arena [əˈriːnə] *n.* 竞技场；表演场地，舞台

counterpart [ˈkaʊntəpɑːt] *n.* 副本；配对物；
　　相对物

purveyor [pəˈveɪə(r)] *n.* 承办商

confirm [kənˈfɜːm] *v.* 证实；[法] 确认，批准

stereotypical [ˌsteriəˈtɪpɪkl] *adj.* 典型的；
　　带有成见的

perception [pəˈsepʃn] *n.* 知觉；观念

compromise [ˈkɒmprəmaɪz] *n.* 妥协

undermining [ˈʌndəmaɪnɪŋ] *v.* 暗中破坏

solidify [səˈlɪdɪfaɪ] *v.* 使凝固，固化

opt [ɒpt] *v.* 选择，挑选

benefit [ˈbenɪfɪt] *n.* 利益，好处

insist on 坚决地宣告；督促；坚持

short-term goals 短期目标

international business 国际商业

foreign investment 外国投资

cross-cultural communication 跨文化交际

an international arena 国际舞台

foreign counterparts 国外同行

back and forth 来回地；一来一往

participate in 分担，参加

wealthy and impersonal 富有而冷漠的

a large multi-million-dollar corporation 一家价
　　值数百万美元的大公司

impersonal purveyor 冷漠的承办商

stereotypical perception 刻板印象

bargain further 进一步讨价还价

✎ **Work individually**：Read the following passage and then paraphrase.

International Business and Cross-cultural Communication

The increase in international business and in foreign investment has created a need for executives with knowledge of foreign languages and skills in cross-cultural communication. Americans, however, have not been well trained in either area and, consequently, have not enjoyed the same level of success in negotiation in an international arena as have their foreign counterparts.

Negotiating is the process of communicating back and forth for the purpose of reaching an agreement. It involves persuasion and compromise, but in order to participate in either one, the negotiators must understand the ways in which people are persuaded and how the compromise is reached within the culture of the negotiation.

In many international business negotiations abroad, Americans are perceived as wealthy and impersonal. It often appears to the foreign negotiators that the American represents a large multi-million-dollar corporation that can afford to pay the price without bargaining further. The American negotiators' role becomes that of an impersonal purveyor of information and cash.

In studies of American negotiators abroad，several traits have been identified that may serve to confirm this stereotypical perception，while undermining the negotiators' position. Two traits in particular that cause cross-cultural misunderstanding is directness and impatience on the part of the American negotiators. Furthermore，American negotiators often insist on realizing short-term goals. Foreign negotiators，on the other hand，may value the relationship established between negotiators and may be willing to invest time in it for long-term benefits. In order to solidify the relationship，they may opt for indirect interactions without regarding for the time involved in getting to know the other negotiator.

Speaking

=== New Words and Phrases ===

attractive [ə'træktɪv] *adj*. 迷人的；有魅力的

commodity [kə'mɒdəti] *n*. 商品；日用品

moderately ['mɒdərətli] *adv*. 适度地；普通地

quotation [kwəʊ'teɪʃn] *n*. 报价（单）

carton ['kɑːtn] *n*. 硬纸盒；塑料盒

catalogue ['kætəlɒg] *n*. 目录

Eastern Garments Co.，Ltd 东方服装有限责任公司

ABC Import & Export Co.，Ltd ABC 进出口有限责任公司

in person 亲自，亲身

in charge of 主管，负责；照料

lady shirt 女士衬衫

before long 不久，很快

HX Series Lady Shirt 哈雪系列女士衬衫

a great deal 大量

take one's time 慢慢来；不慌不忙

to be frank 坦率地说；说实话

come up to 达到；将近

settle the price 结算

be considerate of 体谅

terms of payment 支付条件，付款条件

D/P（documents against payment）付款交单

L/C（Letter of Credit）信用证

Sight L/C（Letter of Credit）即期信用证

take into consideration 考虑到，顾及

make concessions 让步

cut down 减少；裁短；把……砍倒

regular orders 一般的订单；定期订单

smooth transactions 交易顺利进行

shipment and transshipment 装运和转船

assorted colors and sizes 各种颜色和尺码

poly-bag 塑胶袋

Pair work：Listen to the dialogues and have a role play.

=== Dialogue 1 ===

Negotiation Etiquette（1）

A/C: The seller representing The Eastern Garments Co.，Ltd

音频 13 - 3

B/D: The buyer representing ABC Import & Export Co. , Ltd

A: Good afternoon, Miss Chen. Glad to meet you. This is our manager Miss Su.

B: Good afternoon, Miss Lin, Miss Su. It's very nice to see you in person. Let me introduce my colleagues to you. This is Miss Hong. She is in charge of business with clients.

A: How do you do, Miss Hong?

D: How do you do, Miss Lin? Nice to meet you.

A: How are things going?

B: Everything is nice.

A: I hope through your visit we can settle the price for our lady shirt, and conclude the business before long.

B: I think so, Miss Lin. We came here to talk to you about our requirements of HX Series Lady Shirt. Can you show us your price-list and catalogues?

C: We've specially made out a price-list which covers those items most popular on your market. Here you are.

B: Oh, it's very considerate of you. Excuse me. I'll go over your price-list right now.

A: Take your time, Miss Chen.

Dialogue 2

Negotiation Etiquette（2）

音频 13 - 4

B: Oh, Miss Lin. After going over your price-list and catalogues, we are interested in Art No. HX110 and HX 120, but we found that your prices are too higher than those offered by other suppliers. It would be impossible for us to push any sales at such high prices.

C: I'm sorry to hear that. You must know that the cost of production has risen a great deal in recent years while our prices of lady shirt basically remain unchanged. To be frank, our commodities have always come up to our export standard and the packages are excellently designed and printed. So our products are moderately priced.

D: I'm afraid I can't agree with you in this respect. I know that your products are attractive in design, but I wish to point out that your offers are higher than some of the quotations. I've received from your competitors in other countries. So, your price is not competitive in this market.

A: Miss Chen, as you may know, our products which are of high quality have found a good market in many countries. So you must take quality into consideration, too.

音频 13-5

Dialogue 3

Negotiation Etiquette（3）

B: I agree with what you say, but the price difference should not be so big. If you want to get the order, you'll have to lower the price. That's reasonable, isn't it?

A: Well, in order to help you develop business in this line, we may consider making some concessions in your price, but never to that extent.

D: If you are prepared to cut down your price by 8%, we might come to terms.

A: Miss Chen, I can assure you that our price is most favorable. We are sorry to say that we can't bring our price down a lower level.

B: OK, I accept.

Dialogue 4

音频 13-6

Negotiation Etiquette（4）

B: Now let's talk about the terms of payment. Would you accept D/P? I hope it will be acceptable to you.

C: The terms of payment we usually adopt are sight L/C.

D: But I think it would be beneficial to both of us to adopt more flexible payment terms such as D/P terms.

C: Payment by L/C is our usual practice of doing business with all customers for such commodities. I'm sorry we can't accept D/P terms.

D: As for regular orders in future, couldn't you agree to D/P?

A: Sure. After several smooth transactions, we can try D/P terms.

B: Well, as for shipment, the sooner, the better.

A: Yes, shipment is to be made in November, not allowing partial shipment and transshipment.

B: OK, I see. How about packing the goods?

C: We'll pack all the goods in cartons of ten pieces each, assorted colors and sizes per piece in poly-bag. Do you think so?

B: Well, I hope the packing will be attractive.

Unit 14 Farewell Etiquette

Objectives

In this unit, the students are required to grasp the following contents.

1. Learning to talk something about farewell etiquette with some given useful words and phrases of this unit freely.

2. Learning to talk something about farewell etiquette with some given useful sentences of this unit freely.

3. Reading a passage about sending off speech and then paraphrasing it.

4. Listening and having a role play about farewell etiquette.

······ Part I Preparing ······

 Work individually: What do you like to say when you want to leave?

You want to leave, you like to say that ...	Often	Sometimes	Never
I have an engagement soon.			
I think I should go now.			
I'll see you in a couple of days.			
I really must be going. It's rather late.			
I really have to go. I've got a lot to do this morning.			
I will see you tomorrow.			

 Pair work: Compare your answers with a partner.

Usually, what do you say if you want to leave from a party?

······ Part II Performing ······

Reading

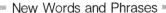

New Words and Phrases

farewell [ˌfeə'wel] n. 告别

impression [ɪm'preʃn] n. 印象

unforgettable [ˌʌnfə'getəbl] adj. 难忘的

gratitude ['grætɪtjuːd] n. 感激

cooperation [kəʊˌɒpə'reɪʃn] n. 合作，协作

punctual ['pʌŋktʃuəl] adj. 准时的

occasion [ə'keɪʒn] n. 场合

applause [ə'plɔːz] n. 鼓掌

attentive [ə'tentɪv] adj. 专注的，留心的

claim [kleɪm] v. 领取

add [æd] v. 补充说

distant ['dɪstənt] adj. 远的

memory ['meməri] n. 记忆，记忆力

observe [əb'zɜːv] v. 观察，查看

beyond [bɪ'jɒnd] prep. 超过

recognition [ˌrekəg'nɪʃn] n. 识别

meanwhile ['miːnwaɪl] adv. 同时

humble ['hʌmbl] adj. 卑下的；低微的；谦逊的

convey [kən'veɪ] v. 表达；转达

profound [prə'faʊnd] adj. 深切的

scholar ['skɒlə(r)] n. 学者

harmonious [hɑː'məʊnɪəs] adj. 和谐的

minority [maɪ'nɒrəti] n. 少数民族

shuttle ['ʃʌtl] v. 穿梭

wonderful ['wʌndəfl] adj. 美妙；极好的，精彩的

mention ['menʃ(ə)n] v. 提到

aspect ['æspekt] n. 方面

gratitude ['grætɪtjuːd] n. 感谢

souvenir [ˌsuːvə'nɪə(r)] n. 纪念品

send-off 送行；送别

take care 保重

give/send one's regards to sb. 代问（某人）好

remember to sb. 代问（某人）好

keep in touch with sb. 与（某人）保持联系

Seeing is believing. 眼见为实。

bid someone farewell 与……告别

on behalf of 代表

How time flies! 时光飞逝。

express our warm send-off to 热烈欢送

propose a toast to 提议为……干杯

distinguished guest 尊贵的客人

international airport 国际机场

terminal building 机场大楼

waiting hall 候机大厅

information desk/inquiry desk 问讯处

departure time /take-off time 起飞时间

arrival time 抵达时间

security check 安全检查

the customs 海关

the boarding pass 登机牌

Group work：Read the following sentences and learn how to use them freely.

1. We are now here again to bid Prof. Smith farewell.

   现在我们又在这里欢送史密斯教授。

103

2. We feel very sorry to see you leave Shanghai. 你就要离开上海了，我们很难过。

3. We feel great regretful at parting with you. 就要与你分别了，我们深感不舍。

4. We enjoyed every minute that we worked with you.
与你们共事的分分秒秒，我们都非常愉快。

5. Your kindness has left a deep impression on us. 你的友善给我们留下了深刻的印象。

6. I want to take this opportunity to ask Prof. Smith to convey our best regards to his people.
我想借此机会请史密斯教授向他的同胞转达我们的良好祝愿。

7. May our friendship last forever! 愿我们的友谊长存！

8. Wish you a pleasant journey. 祝你旅途愉快。

9. I wish you every success in your work. 祝你事业有成。

10. Then allow me to take this opportunity to say goodbye to you.
然后请允许我利用这个机会向你们道别。

11. Several days ago, we met as strangers; today we say goodbye to each other as friends.
几天前当我们相遇时还彼此陌生，然而今天我们告别时却已成为朋友。

12. A good friend from afar brings a distant land closer. 海内存知己，天涯若比邻。

13. Nothing is more delightful than to meet friends from afar. 有朋自远方来，不亦乐乎！

14. When you come back in the future, our country may have changed beyond recognition.
当你将来再回来时，我们的国家可能变得让你认不出来了。

15. Once again, thank you for your cooperation and support.
再次感谢你们的合作与支持。

Listening 🎧

─────── **Useful Expressions** ───────

farewell dinner 散伙饭   plane ticket 机票

have a good rest 好好休息   see sb. off 为某人送行

a very enjoyable stay 过得很愉快

 Pair work： Listen to the dialogues and fill in the blanks.

─────── Dialogue 1 ───────

After the Farewell Dinner

音频 14-1

A: How time _____! You're leaving tomorrow. We wish you could _____ longer.

B: Thank you for your _____ and your dinner. And thank you for all your help _____ _____ my stay here.

A: Don't _____ it. It's a great _____ to help you. Here is your plane ticket. The plane will take _____ at 9:00. I'll drive a car to pick you _____ at 7:00 at your hotel and see you _____ at the airport tomorrow morning. Is that OK?

B: Oh, it's very kind of you. I'll be ready.

A: Well, it's getting late. I think you'd better have a good rest tonight. You'll be having a tiring _____ tomorrow.

B: OK. See you tomorrow.

━━━━━ Dialogue 2 ━━━━━

Seeing off at the Airport

音频 14 - 2

A: It's very _____ of you to come to see me off.

B: My pleasure. I'm sorry you've got to _____ us. We will miss you.

A: Me too. During my stay in China, you and your colleagues have shown me your great ____ _____ in every _____. I really don't know how to express my gratitude.

B: I'm happy to do what I can. We've both enjoyed our relationship, haven't we?

A: Yes, I have had a very enjoyable stay in China. I've met so many _____ Chinese friends. I've learnt a lot from them.

B: I'm so happy that you have loved our country.

A: Before I came here, I only had an _____ of China from books, newspapers, TV and the Internet. Now I've seen China with my own eyes.

B: "Seeing is believing." It's more important to learn from _____ life. I'm so sorry that we didn't have enough time to visit Shaoxing. Come to China again if you have time. You're always welcome.

A: Thank you. I hope we'll _____ in touch.

B: So do I.

A: They're starting to _____ luggage. I got to go. Goodbye.

B: Goodbye. Wish you a nice trip home, and please send my best _____ to your family.

•••••• **Part III   Practicing** ••••••

Reading

━━━━━ New Words and Phrases ━━━━━

sincere [sɪnˈsɪə(r)] *adj.* 真诚的，诚挚的   ┆ give sb. a warm welcome 热烈欢迎某人

say good-bye to sb. 跟某人告别

make great contributions to 为……做出巨大的贡献

effective methods 有效的方法

written English 英语书面语

spoken English 英语口语

communicative abilities 交际能力

as a result of 由于……的结果

bid farewell to 与……告辞

Work individually：Read the following passage and then paraphrase.

A Send-off Speech

Boys and girls，

We still remember that one year ago，it was just here that we gave Professor Smith a warm welcome. Now we gather here once again to say good-bye to him.

During the past year，Professor Smith has made great contributions to the improvement of English teaching quality of our school. He has brought to us not only effective methods but also new ideas of how to balance the learning of written English and that of spoken English. It's obvious that the English communicative abilities of our students have improved a great deal as a result of Professor Smith's efforts. During the last year，Professor Smith and our students and teachers have become good friends. We feel sorry that we have to say good-bye now，but I'm sure we will remember each other forever.

Now in bidding farewell to Professor Smith，allow me on behalf of all the students and teachers of our school to express our sincere thanks to him and I would also like to take this opportunity to wish him a pleasant safe journey home.

Speaking

New Words and Phrases

preparedness [prɪˈpeədnəs] *n.* 有准备，已准备

terminal [ˈtɜːmɪnl] *n.* 候机楼

have a good sleeping 睡个好觉

take an umbrella 带上雨伞

as an old saying goes 俗话说

There is no danger when there is preparedness. 有备无患。

check out 检查

at the dining room 在餐厅

make the payment 支付

credit card 信用卡

visa card 维萨卡

take a print of 打印

a heavy traffic 交通繁忙

international terminal 国际候机楼

Pair work：Listen to the dialogues and have a role play.

音频 14 - 3

Dialogue 1

Greeting

A: Good morning，Miss Zhang! Did you have a good sleep?

B: Yes，good.

A: Have you packed?

B: I am packing now.

A: En，I think you should take an umbrella. As an old saying goes，"There is no danger when there is preparedness."

B: Yes. The weather is changeable.

A: If you're ready，we can go and check out.

B: OK. Let's go.

音频 14 - 4

Dialogue 2

Checking Out

H: Good morning. How can I help you?

B: Excuse me. I will leave today. I'd like to pay my bill now.

H: OK，your name and your room number，please?

B: Zhang Hui，113.

H: Have you used any hotel services this morning or had breakfast at the hotel dining room，Miss Zhang?

B: Yes，I just had breakfast at the dining room，but I didn't use any services.

H: OK. Your bill totals 120 dollars.

B: I see.

H: How would you like to make the payment，Miss Zhang?

B: Credit card. May I use my visa card?

H: Yes. Let me take a print of your card.

B: Here it is.

H: Please wait a moment. Sorry to have kept you waiting. Please sign on the print.

B: OK.

H: Thank you. Here's your receipt.

B: Thank you.

音频 14 - 5

Dialogue 3

On Board the Car

B: Wow，there is heavy traffic.

A: Yes. So we must pay more attention to avoid missing the plane.

B: Yes, you are right.

A: I'd like to thank you for coming, and I hope you enjoyed your time during the journey. Do you have any questions about the things we shared with you during our factory tour?

B: No, your explanation was quite thorough, and I pretty much saw all that we came to see. Thank you for spending the afternoon with us.

A: It was my pleasure! Well, if you don't have any questions now, but think of something later, please don't hesitate to email me.

B: Thanks! We'll be sure to keep in touch.

A: Yes.

B: How long is the ride?

A: About half an hour.

B: En... It should be in time.

A: There is a magazine in the back of the seat. You can read it.

B: OK, thank you.

 Dialogue 4

In the Airport

音频 14 - 6

A: Here we are. This is the airport.

B: Here I must say good-bye to you.

A: I'm sorry to see you off. What airline are you flying with?

B: Um... Let me look at the ticket... Oh, Japan Air.

A: Japan Air is in terminal B. This is the international terminal, so all you have to do is to walk straight through those doors and turn to your left, and you should see the check-in counter.

B: Thanks again for all your help.

A: Is there anything else I can do for you before your departure?

B: No. I appreciate everything you have done for me. I really don't know how to thank you.

A: Don't mention it. I'm sure your visit will help to promote the friendship and understanding between both of us. Here's a present for you.

B: I really appreciate all of your hospitality. I'm looking forward to your visiting Japan.

A: I promise I'll take the first chance to call on you when I get there.

B: OK. Let's keep in touch.

Module 4

International Trade Situation

Unit 15 Establishing Relationship

In this unit, the students are required to grasp the following contents.

1. Learning to talk something about establishing relationship with some given useful words and phrases of this unit freely.
2. Learning to talk something about establishing relationship with some given useful sentences of this unit freely.
3. Reading a letter of establishing relationship and then paraphrasing it.
4. Listening and having a role play about establishing relationship.

······· Part I   Preparing ·······

 Work individually: What contents does establishing relationship include?

About establishing relationship	Often	Sometimes	Never
No customer, no business			
Establishing business relations is the first step in transaction in foreign trade			
It is important to establish business relations			
Channels and methods for establishing business relations			
Chambers of Commerce both at home and abroad			
Tactics of establishing business relations			

 Pair work: Compare your answers with a partner.

Do you know how to establish relationship about international trade?

······· Part II　Performing ·······

Reading

New Words and Phrases

deal [di:l] *n.* 交易	trade agreement 贸易协议
handle ['hændl] *v.* 经营	business association 业务联系
commodity [kə'mɒdəti] *n.* 商品	business connection 业务联系
consignment [kən'saɪnmənt] *n.* 装运的货物	foreign trade 对外贸易
container [kən'teɪnə(r)] *n.* 货柜；货箱	overseas trade 海外贸易
copyright ['kɒpɪraɪt] *n.* 版权	international trade 国际贸易
creditor ['kredɪtə(r)] *n.* 债权人	trade with 和……进行贸易
default [dɪ'fɔːlt] *n.* 违约；拖欠	do business in a moderate way 做生意稳重
deficit ['defɪsɪt] *n.* 赤字；亏损	do business in a sincere way 做生意诚恳
devaluation [diːˌvæljʊ'eɪʃn] *n.* 贬值	make a deal 做一笔交易
dishonor [dɪs'ɒnə] *n.* 拒付	deal in 经营，做生意
dividend ['dɪvɪdend] *n.* 股息	explore the possibilities of 探讨……的可能性
equity ['ekwəti] *n.* 产权；主权；权益	trade circles 贸易界
business scope/frame 经营范围	trade in 经营某商品
trading firm/house 贸易行，商行	trade prospects/outlook 贸易前景
trade by commodities 商品贸易	trade cooperation 贸易合作
visible trade 有形贸易	technological cooperation 技术合作
invisible trade 无形贸易	business cooperation 业务合作
barter trade 易货贸易	cooperative relationship 合作关系
bilateral trade 双边贸易	the scope of cooperation 合作范围
triangle trade 三角贸易	trade fair 贸易展销会
multilateral trade 多边贸易	trade show 贸易展览
counter trade 对销贸易；抵偿贸易	trade agreement 贸易协议
counter purchase 互购贸易	establish arrangement 达成协议
buy-back 回购贸易	reach an agreement 达成协议
compensation trade 补偿贸易	trade terms/clause 贸易条款
processing trade 来料加工贸易	trade balance 贸易平衡
assembling trade 来料装配贸易	conclude a business transaction 达成贸易交易
leasing trade 租赁贸易	work with 与……共事
in exchange for 用来交换……	business activities 经济活动

business house 商行；商号

trading department 贸易机构

trade association 贸易协会

foreign trade department 对外贸易部门

C. C. P. I. T.（China Council for the Promotion of International Trade）中国国际贸易促进委员会

Chinese Commercial Counselor's Office 中国使馆的商务处

Chamber of Commerce 商会

trading partnership 经营合伙人

foreign trade personnel 外贸工作者

trading center 贸易中心

trading market 贸易市场

tradesman 商人，零售商

close relationship 密切的关系

establish/enter into/set up/business relationship 建立业务关系

continue business relationship 继续业务关系

present business relationship 保持业务关系

improve business relationship 改善业务关系

promote business relationship 促进业务关系

speed up business relationship 加快业务关系的发展

enlarge/widen business relationship 扩大业务关系

restore/resume business relationship 恢复业务关系

interrupt business relationship 中断业务关系

cement business relationship 巩固业务关系

 Group work：Read the following sentences and learn how to use them freely.

1. We've come to know your name and address from the Commercial Counselor's Office of the Chinese Embassy in London. 我们从中国驻伦敦大使馆经济商务参赞处得知你们的名字和地址。

2. By the courtesy of Mr. Black, we are given to understand the name and address of your firm. 承蒙布莱克先生的介绍，我们得知贵公司的名称和地址。

3. We are willing to enter into business relations with your firm.
我们愿意与贵公司建立业务关系。

4. Your firm has been introduced/recommended/passed on to us by Maple Company.
枫叶公司向我方介绍了贵公司。

5. Our mutual understanding and cooperation will certainly result in important business.
我们之间的相互了解与合作必将促成重要的生意。

6. We express our desire to establish business relations with your firm.
我们愿和贵公司建立业务关系。

7. We shall be glad to enter into business relations with you.
我们很乐意同贵公司建立业务关系。

8. We now avail ourselves of this opportunity to write to you with a view to entering into business relations with you. 现在我们借此机会致函贵公司，希望和贵公司建立业务关系。

9. We are now writing you for the purpose of establishing business relations with you.
我们特此致函是想与贵方建立业务关系。

10. Your desire to establish business relations coincides with ours.

你方想同我方建立业务关系的愿望与我方是一致的。

11. We specialize in the export of Japanese light industrial products and would like to trade with you in this line.

鉴于我方专营日本轻工业产品出口业务，我方愿与贵方在这方面开展贸易。

12. Our lines are mainly arts and crafts. 我们经营的商品主要是工艺品。

13. We have been in this line of business for more than twenty years.

我们经营这类商品已有 20 多年的历史了。

14. Your letter expressing the hope of establishing business connections with us has met with approval. 来函收悉，得知贵方愿与我方建立业务关系，我们表示同意。

15. In order to acquaint you with the textiles we handle, we take pleasure in sending you by air our latest catalogue for your perusal.

为了使贵方对我方经营的纺织品有所了解，特航寄我方最新目录，供细阅。

16. Glad to see you in your company. 很高兴在贵公司见到您。

17. It's only half an hour's car ride. 只有半小时的车程。

18. Suppose we make it, say three o'clock tomorrow afternoon.

如果我们能去的话，那么就明天下午三点钟吧。

19. It would be very helpful if you could send us statistics on your sales.

如果你们能将你们的销售统计资料寄给我们，那可就太有帮助了。

20. We would like to ask you to send us the related information.

我们希望你们能将相关资料寄给我们。

Listening 🎧

═══════ Useful Expressions ═══════

coincide [ˌkəʊɪnˈsaɪd] v. 相符；与……一致；想法、意见等相同

pamphlet [ˈpæmflət] n. 小册子；活页文选

reputation [ˌrepjuˈteɪʃn] n. 名气，名声

equality [ɪˈkwɒləti] n. 同等，平等

be known for 以……而闻名

traditional export 传统的出口贸易

financial position 财务状况

credit standing 信誉

trade reputation 贸易信誉；贸易声誉

refer to 参考；指的是；涉及；适用于

local chamber of commerce 地方商会

inquiry agency 询价机构

on the basis of 根据；依据；以……为基础；按照

mutual benefit 互惠互利

definite answer 明确的回答；明确的答复

special answer 特殊的回答

put through 实行；完成；使经历；接通（电话）

on business 出差；因公

Bank of China 中国银行

start business 开始业务
have a glance at 瞥一眼
home and abroad 国内外

IBM（International Business Machines Corporation）国际商业机器公司或万国商业机器公司

 Pair work：Listen to the dialogues and fill in the blanks.

音频 15 - 1

━━ Dialogue 1 ━━

Establishing Relationship（1）

A: I had a look yesterday. I found some exhibits are fine in _____ and beautiful in _____. The exhibition has successfully _____ to me what your _____ handles. I have gone over the _____ and the _____ enclosed in your last letter. I have got some idea of your _____. I am interested in your _____ blouses.

B: Our silks are known for their _____. They are one of our _____ exports. Silk blouses are brightly colored and beautifully designed. They are greatly _____ overseas and are always in great _____.

A: Some of them are of the latest _____. Now I have a feeling that we can do a lot of trade in this _____. We wish to establish _____ with you.

B: Your _____ coincides with ours.

A: Concerning our _____ position，_____ and _____，you may refer to our bank, or to our local _____ of commerce or inquiry agencies.

B: Thank you for your _____. As you know, our corporation is a _____ one. We always trade with foreign countries on the basis of _____ and _____. I have no doubt that it will bring about _____ between us.

A: That sounds interesting！I will send a fax. As soon as I receive the definite answer，I will give you _____.

B: We will make an offer as soon as possible. I hope a lot of business will be _____ between us.

A: So do I.

B: I hope everything will be _____.

A: That is _____ I want to say.

B: I will give you the lowest price in the _____.

A: Thank you！

━━ Dialogue 2 ━━

Establishing Relationship（2）

音频 15 - 2

A: Welcome to our _____，Mr. Johnson. My name is Yan Hua，the _____ of Mr. Wang.

B: Thank you.

A: Would you like to have a cup of tea or _____?

B: Thanks. I like _____ very much.

A: Glad you like it. By the _____, is this your first visit to China，Mr. Johnson?

B: Yes，as a representative of _____, I hope to conclude some _____ with you.

A: We also hope to _____ our business with you.

B: This is our _____ desire.

A: I think you probably know China has adopted a _____ policy in her _____ trade.

B: Yes, I've heard about it，but I'd like to know _____ about it.

A: Right. Seeing is _____.

B: Sure.

········· **Part III   Practicing** ·······

Reading

═══════ New Words and Phrases ═══════

confectioner [kənˈfekʃənə(r)] *n.* 糖果制造
人，糖果店

baker [ˈbeɪkə(r)] *n.* 面包店

extensive [ɪkˈstensɪv] *adj.* 广阔的，广大
的；范围广泛的

quotation [kwəʊˈteɪʃn] *n.* 行情，行市；行市
表，估价单

unreliability [ˌʌnrɪˌlaɪəˈbɪləti] *n.* 不安全性，
不可靠性

alleviate [əˈliːvieɪt] *v.* 减轻，缓和

apricot [ˈeɪprɪkɒt] *n.* 杏；杏树；杏仁

kernel [ˈkɜːnl] *n.* 核；核心；要点；谷粒

flavor [ˈfleɪvə] *n.* 味；香料；韵味

extensive connection 广泛的连接

a regular supply 定期供应

commission house 可提取佣金的商行

frequent fluctuations of price 价格的经常波动

a direct connection 直接联系

in large quantities 大量地

specific enquiries 具体询盘

a competitive price 有竞争力的价格

trade terms and conditions 贸易的一般交易
条件，贸易条款

business status 营业状况，业务情况

Work individually： Read the following passage and then paraphrase.

A Letter of Establishing Business Relations

Dear Sirs，

    This is to introduce ourselves as confectioners and bakers having many years' experience in this particular line of business. Our firm，located at the east end of Copenhagen，was established nearly half a century ago and has extensive connections with food stores in the cities and towns. We need a regular supply of bitter apricot kernels for cakes and candies. Up to now, we have been buying from the commission houses, which used to send us quotations regularly. There have been of late, frequent fluctuations of price and unreliability in the matter of supply. It is an attempt to alleviate this situation that we are seeking to establish a direct connection with your corporation, for we prefer Chinese apricot kernels above all for their fine quality and special flavor.

We take the liberty of writing to you with a view to establishing business relations with you and meanwhile asking you to make us an offer at a competitive price for 50 metric tons of bitter apricot kernels, September shipment, together with your trade terms and conditions. For your information, we are also interested in other kinds of Chinese nuts in large quantities and send you specific enquiries later on.

As to our financial standing, we wish to refer you to our bank, Jardine Matheaon Bank, 57 Waterloo Street Copenhagen, who we feel sure will be glad to furnish you with any information that you may require. In case you need more information about our business status, we shall be only too glad to answer your inquires at any time.

Yours faithfully,

LiLy

Speaking 🎤

==== New Words and Phrases ====

coinsurance [ˌkəʊɪnˈʃʊərəns] *n.* 共负保险

collateral [kəˈlætərəl] *n.* 抵押品

dividend [ˈdɪvɪdend] *n.* 股息

drawee [drɔːˈiː] *n.* 受票人

drawer [drɔː(r)] *n.* 发票人

freight [freɪt] *n.* 运费

goodwill [ˌɡʊdˈwɪl] *n.* 商誉

absolute advantage 绝对优势

American Chamber of Commerce in Hong Kong 香港美国商会

authorized capital 注册股本；法定股本

automatic credit transfer 自动转账收款

automatic teller machine 自动柜员机

average clause 受保范围；损失条款

avoidable risk 可避免之风险

bad debt 呆账；坏账

balance of payments 国际收支差额

balance of trade 国际贸易差额

balance sheet 资产负债表

bank credit 银行信用

bank draft 银行汇票

bank interest rate 银行利率

bank note 钞票

bank overdraft 银行透支

bank service 银行服务

bear market 熊市；淡市

best lending rate 最优惠贷款利率；最优惠利率

bilateral arrangement 双边协议

bill of exchange 汇票

bill of lading 提货单

bill payable 应付票据

bill receivable 应收票据

 Pair work：Listen to the dialogues and have a role play.

━━ Dialogue 1 ━━

音频 15 - 3

Establishing Relationship（3）

A: Would you like to have a look at our showroom，Ms Olive?

B: I'd like to.

A: This way，please.

B: Thank you. How beautiful!

A: Where shall we start?

B: It will take hours if I really take a look at everything.

A: You may be interested in some of our items. Let's look at those.

B: Good idea. I can just have plans and a rest.

A: By the way，Ms Olive. How long have you been in this business?

B: I have been in this business for more than 20 years.

A: No wonder you are so experienced.

B: Our business has become difficult since competition grows.

A: That's true.

B: Do you have a catalogue or something that can tell me about your company?

A: Yes，I will get you some later.

B: Thanks. When can we work for a deal?

A: Would tomorrow be convenient?

B: Yes，it will be fine.

━━ Dialogue 2 ━━

音频 15 - 4

Establishing Relationship（4）

D: Here is our sample room.

G: You certainly have got a large collection of sample foodstuffs here.

D: Yes. We are exporting a wide range of foodstuffs to many countries. And the demand is getting greater and greater.

G: So it is. Though we haven't done business with you，as you know，your exports of foodstuffs to our country have considerably increased during the last few years. It appears that Chinese foodstuffs are very attractive.

D: You said it. The quality of ours is as good as that of many other suppliers，while our prices are not high as theirs. By the way，which items are you interested in?

117

G: Canned goods are of special interest to me，particularly the canned fruit and meat. As your canned fruit is among the most popular ones in our market，I'm going to place an order in a day or two.

D: Good. How about our canned meat?

G: I think it will also find a good marketing in our country. Will you show me some samples?

D: Yes. This way, please! Our canned meat comes in various weighs. The largest one weighs three and a half pounds net, the smallest seven ounces net.

G: The small sizes are more saleable in our market than the large ones. I've brought with me a sample of canned meat which is only six ounces. The smallest size of yours is even bigger than that of mine. I wonder if your canned meat tastes better.

D: You are welcome to have a try. Here it is. Ours is of prime quality.

G: Oh，it's delicious. Mm... I'm not sure about the pesticide residues in your foodstuffs, though I'm sure you must have given much thought to the matter. But you know, our governmental restrictions have been getting more and more tight，so we are not allowed to import any polluted goods.

D: You can rest assured. Our foodstuffs are guaranteed to conform to WHO standards.

G: Good. I'd like to order meat of this kind in seven ounce tins if the price is competitive.

D: What about other canned goods, such as canned mushrooms and vegetables?

G: They are not as saleable as canned fruit，I suppose.

D: Mm，no. I really do not think so. They are also among our major exports and have found a favorable reception in many other countries.

G: Then，may I have a look at the samples first?

D: Certainly. Here you are.

G: Ah，very nice indeed. But I am not sure whether they are to the taste of our people. What would you say to my taking some samples home before I make a decision?

D: That's all right.

G: Well，I have an appointment at 4:00. Shall we talk about it tomorrow morning ?

D: OK. See you tomorrow.

G: Goodbye!

Unit 16 Enquiry and Quotation

In this unit, the students are required to grasp the following contents.

1. Learning to talk something about enquiry and quotation with some given useful words and phrases of this unit freely.

2. Learning to talk something about enquiry and quotation with some given useful sentences of this unit freely.

3. Reading a letter of an order and then paraphrasing it.

4. Listening and having a role play about quotation.

.... Part I Preparing ......

Work individually: What contents does enquiry include?

About enquiry	Often	Sometimes	Never
Definition of inquiry			
Inquiry process			
Inquiry is an approach to learning that involves a process of exploring the natural or material world			
Inquiry leads to asking questions and making discoveries			
Inquiry can test those discoveries in the search for new understanding			
Inquiry, as it relates to science education, should mirror as closely as possible the enterprise of doing real science			

 Pair work: Compare your answers with a partner.

Do you know anything about inquiry and quotation?

⋯⋯⋯ Part II Performing ⋯⋯⋯

Reading

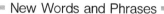 New Words and Phrases

hover ['hɒvə(r)] v. 徘徊于⋯⋯，盘旋于

moderately ['mɒdərətli] adv. 适当地，合适地；适度地

utmost ['ʌtməʊst] n. 极限，竭尽所能

economically [ˌiːkə'nɒmɪkli] adv. 经济地，便宜地

acceptable [ək'septəbl] adj. 可以接受的，可以使用的

ceiling price 最高价，顶价

maximum price 最高价

minimum price 最低价

average price 平均价格

base price 底价

rock bottom price 最低价

bedrock price 最低价

original price 原价

stainless steel 不锈钢

cost level 成本费用的水平

exchange rate 汇率

price terms 价格条款

free on board（FOB）船上交货价，离岸价格

cost，insurance and freight（CIF）成本加保险费、运费，到岸价格

cost and freight（C/F）成本加运费，离岸加运费

FOB liner terms f. o. b. 班轮条件

FOB stowed 船上交货并理舱

FOB trimmed 船上交货并平舱

FOB under tackle f. o. b. 吊钩下交货

CIF liner terms c. i. f. 班轮条件

CIF ex ship's hold c. i. f. 舱底交货

FOB plane 飞机离岸价（用于紧急情况）

pass over 转给，转嫁

free on rail（for）火车交货价

free on truck（fot）汽车交货价

free alongside ship（fas）船边交货价

ex factory 工厂交货价

ex plantation 农场交货价

ex warehouse 仓库交货价

ex ship 目的港船上交货价

ex dock duty paid 目的港码头完税交货价

ex dock duty unpaid 目的港码头未完税交货价

buying price 买价

selling price 卖价

new price 新价

old price 旧价

present price 现价

original price 原价

current price 时价，现价

prevailing price 现价

ruling price 目前的价格

going price 现价

opening price 开价，开盘价

closing price 收盘价

exceptional price 特价

special price 特价

nominal price 有行无市的价格

moderate price 公平价格

wholesale price 批发价

retail price 零售价

market price 市价

net price 净价

cost price 成本价

gross price 毛价

price effect 价格效应

price contract 价格合约

price calculation 价格计算

price limit 价格限制

price control 价格控制

price theory 价格理论

price regulation 价格调整

price structure 价格构成

extra price 附加价

price ratio 比价

price per unit 单价

price index/price indices 物价指数

price of factory 厂价

 Group work：Read the following sentences and learn how to use them freely.

1. Heavy enquiries witness the quality of our products.

   大量询盘证明我们的产品质量过硬。

2. As soon as the price picks up, enquiries will revive.　一旦价格回升，询盘将恢复活跃。

3. Enquiries for carpets are getting more numerous.　对地毯的询盘日益增加。

4. Enquiries are so large that we can only allot you 200 cases.

   询盘如此之多，我们只能分给你们 200 箱货。

5. Enquiries are dwindling.　询盘正在减少。

6. Enquiries are dried up.　询盘正在绝迹。

7. They promised to transfer their future enquiries to Chinese corporations.

   他们答应将以后的询盘转给中国公司。

8. Generally speaking, inquiries are made by the buyers.　询盘一般由买方发出。

9. Mr. Baker is sent to Beijing to make an inquiry at China National Textiles Corporation.

   贝克先生来北京向中国纺织品总公司进行询价。

10. We regret that the goods you inquire about are not available.

    很遗憾，你们所询的货物现在无货。

11. In the import and export business, we often make inquiries at foreign suppliers.

    在进出口交易中，我们常向外商询价。

12. To make an inquiry about our oranges, a representative of the Japanese company paid us

    a visit.　为了对我们的橙子询价，那家日本公司的一名代表访问了我们。

13. We cannot take care of your enquiry at present.　我们现在无力顾及你方的询盘。

14. Your enquiry is too vague to enable us to reply you.　你们的询盘不明确，我们无法答复。

15. Now that we've already made an inquiry about your articles, will you please reply as soon

as possible? 既然我们已经对你们的产品询价，可否尽快给予答复？

16. China Silk Corporation received the inquiry sheet sent by a British company.
中国中丝集团有限公司收到了英国一家公司的询价单。

17. Could you please send us a catalog of your rubber boots together with terms of payment?
你能给我们寄一份胶靴的目录和付款方式吗？

18. He inquired about the varieties, specifications and price, and so on.
他询问了品种、花色和价格等情况。

19. We have inquired of Manager Zhang about the varieties, quality and price of tea.
我们向张经理询问了茶叶的品种、质量、价格等问题。

20. Would you accept delivery spread over a period of time?
不知你们能不能接受在一段时间里分批交货？

21. If your prices are favorable, I can place the order right away.
如果你们的价格优惠，我们可以马上订货。

Listening 🎧

━━━━ Useful Expressions ━━━━

free trade zone 自由贸易区

value of foreign trade 对外贸易值

value of international trade 国际贸易值

generalized system of preferences（GSP）普遍优惠制

most-favored nation treatment（MFNT）最惠国待遇

a ready market 现成的市场

be subject to 受支配；从属于；可以……的；常遭受……

general practice 惯例

international general practice 国际惯例

commodity inspection 商品检验

as a rule 照例；通常，一般说来；照说

sales department 销售部，营业部

a great deal 大量

business scope 营业范围

ever before 以前

quite a bit 相当多

Pair work：Listen to the dialogues and fill in the blanks.

音频 16 - 1

━━━━ Dialogue 1 ━━━━

Inquiry（1）

Tom: I'm glad to have the chance to visit your _____. I hope to conclude some substantial _____ with you.

Chen: It's great pleasure. Mr. Tom, to have the opportunity of meeting you, I believe you have seen the exhibits in the _____ . May I know what particular _____ you are interested in?

Tom: I'm interested in your _____ . I have seen the exhibits and studied your _____ . I think some of the items will find _____ in Holland. Here is a list of my _____ , for which I'd like to have your lowest quotations, _____ Sydney.

Chen: Thank you for your _____ . Would you tell us the _____ you require so as to enable us to _____ the offers?

Tom: I'll do that. Meanwhile, would you give me an _____ of price?

Chen: Here are our FOB price lists. All the prices in the lists are _____ to our confirmation.

Tom: What about the _____ ? From European suppliers I usually get a 3 to 5 percent commission for my imports. It's the _____ .

Chen: As a _____ we do not _____ any commission. But if the order is large enough, we'll _____ it.

Tom: You see, I do business on commission basis. A commission on your _____ would make it easier for me to _____ sales. Even a 2 or 3 percent would help.

Chen: We'll _____ this when you place your _____ with us.

========= Dialogue 2 =========

Inquiry（2）

音频 16 - 2

A: Good afternoon. I am Mr. Brown, the import manager of _____ Ltd, Sydney, Australia. This is my _____ .

B: Good afternoon, Mr. Brown. My name is Mrs. Anderson, _____ of the sales department.

A: Nice to see you, Mrs. Anderson.

B: Nice to see you too, Mr. Brown. Won't you _____ ?

A: Thank you.

B: What would you like, _____ or _____ ?

A: I'd prefer coffee if you don't _____ .

B: Is it your first trip to the _____ , Mr. Brown?

A: No, it's the _____ time.

B: Good. Is there _____ you find changed about the Fair?

A: Yes, a great deal. The _____ has been broadened, and there are more visitors than _____ .

B: Really，Mr. Brown? Did you find anything _____ ?

A: Oh，yes. _____ . But we are especially interested in your _____ .

B: We are glad to hear that. What items are you _____ interested in?

A: Women's dresses. They are _____ and suit Australian women well，too. If they are of high _____ and the prices are _____ ，we'll purchase large quantities of them. Will you please quote us a _____ ?

B: All right.

⋯⋯⋯⋯ Part III   Practicing ⋯⋯⋯⋯

Reading

==================== New Words and Phrases ====================

import ['ɪmpɔːt] *n.* 输入；进口 *v.* 输入，进口

export ['ekspɔːt] *n.* 输出，出口 *v.* 出口，输出

technology [tek'nɒlədʒi] *n.* 技术，科技（总称）

impress [ɪm'pres] *v.* 给……以深刻印象

selection [sɪ'lekʃn] *n.* 选择

chain [tʃeɪn] *n.* 链子，链条；连锁

retailer ['riːteɪlə(r)] *n.* 零售商，零售店

manufacturer [ˌmænju'fæktʃərə(r)] *n.* 制造商，制造厂

range [reɪndʒ] *n.* 范围；射程

teenage ['tiːneɪdʒ] *adj.* 十几岁的；青少年的

normally ['nɔːməli] *adv.* 正常地；通常地

garment ['gɑːmənt] *n.* 服装；衣服

current ['kʌrənt] *adj.* 现在的；最近的

a wide range of 范围广泛的；大范围的；广泛的

teenage market 青少年市场

in addition to 除……之外

terms of payment 支付条件，付款条件

at one time 一度，从前

price list 价格表

Work individually：Read the following passage and then paraphrase.

A Letter of an Order

Chifeshel Import and Export Trade Corporation

Import and Export Trade Corporation

18F Trade Building，Fenghuang Road，

Xiangzhou，Zhuhai，China

December 10th 2016

Our Ref. CFE/520

Your Ref. ZML/HD202/183/004

Chifeshel Import and Export Trade Corporation

Beijing Institute of Technology. Zhuhai

6 Jinfeng Road Tangjiawan

Zhuhai China

Dear Sirs,

We were impressed by the selection of lights that were displayed on your stand at the Exhibition that was held in Guangzhou last month.

We are a large chain of retailers and looking for a manufacturer who could supply us with a wide range of lights for the teenage market.

As we usually place very large orders, we would expect a quantity discount in addition to a 20% trade discount off net list prices, and our terms of payment are normally 30 days bill of exchange, documents against payment.

If these conditions interest you, and you can meet orders of over 1,000 garments at one time, please send us your current catalogue and price list. We hope to hear from you soon.

Yours faithfully,

Zhangjunju

Sales manager

Speaking 🎤

========= New Words and Phrases =========

delivery [dɪˈlɪvəri] *n.* 交货

offer [ˈɒfə(r)] *n.* 报盘

catalogue [ˈkætəlɒg] *n.* 目录

counteroffer [ˈkaʊntəɔːfə] *n.* 还盘

regret [rɪˈgret] *n.* 遗憾

reduce [rɪˈdjuːs] *v.* 减少，降低

accept [əkˈsept] *v.* 接受

acceptance [əkˈseptəns] *n.* 接受

sign [saɪn] *v.* 签名

signature [ˈsɪgnətʃə(r)] *n.* 签名

first inquiry 初次询价

general inquiry 一般询价

specific inquiry 具体询价

effect delivery 装运

all necessary information 所有必要的信息

delivery date 装运期

voluntary offer 主动报盘

free offer 虚盘（自由报盘）

firm offer 实盘

pro forma invoice 形式发票

import license 进口许可证

under cover 随函附上

supply from stock 供现货

be on the high side 偏高

be in line with 与……相符

the prevailing market 行市

confirmation of order 订单的确认

sales contract 销售合同

purchase contract 购买合同

sales confirmation 销售确认书

purchase confirmation 供货确认书

counter-signature 会签

specialize in 专营

meet with great favor 大受欢迎

the latest catalogue 最新目录

the latest price list 最新价目表

 Pair work：Listen to the dialogues and have a role play.

 **Dialogue 1**

Quotation（1）

音频 16 - 3

A: Have you worked out the offers，Mr. Zhou?

B: Yes，we have. Here's our CIF quotation sheet. Please have a careful look.

A: Are the prices on the list firm offers?

B: Yes. All the quotations on the list are subject to our final confirmation.

A: I wonder whether there are any changes in your prices.

B: All these products are our best-selling lines. The prices of our products will change according to that of the international market demand. And we are always open to negotiate，especially on larger orders. What do you have in mind?

A: How long does your offer remain valid? I need some time to get my supervisors on board with this plan.

B: I understand. Our offer remains open for 4 days.

Dialogue 2

Quotation（2）

音频 16 - 4

A: I have here our price sheet on a FOB basis. The prices are given without engagement.

B: Good. If you excuse me，I'll go over the sheet right now.

A: Take your time.

B: I can tell you at a glance that your prices are much too high.

A: I'm surprised to hear you say so. You know that the cost of production has been skyrocketing in recent years.

B: We only ask that your prices be comparable to others. That's reasonable，isn't it?

A: Well，to get the business done，we can consider making some concessions in our prices. But first，you'll have to give me an idea of the quantity you wish to order from us，so that we may adjust our prices accordingly.

B: The size of our order depends greatly on the prices. Let's settle that matter first.

A: Well, as I've said, if your order is large enough, we're ready to reduce our prices by 2 percent.

B: When I say your prices are much too high, I don't mean they are higher merely by 2 or 3 percent.

A: How much do you mean then? Can you give me a rough idea?

B: To have this business concluded, I should say a reduction of at least 10 percent would help.

A: Impossible. How can you expect us to make a reduction to that extent?

B: I think you are as well-informed as I am about the market for chemical fertilizers. It's unnecessary for me to point out that supply exceeds demand at present and that this situation is apt to continue for a long time yet. May I suggest that you call your home office and see what they have to say?

A: Very well, I will.

Unit 17 Business Negotiation

In this unit, the students are required to grasp the following contents.

1. Learning to talk something about business negotiation with some given useful words and phrases of this unit freely.

2. Learning to talk something about business negotiation with some given useful sentences of this unit freely.

3. Reading a passage about business negotiation and then paraphrasing it.

4. Listening and having a role play about price discussion.

······ Part I   Preparing ······

 Work individually: What contents does the business negotiation include?

About business negotiation	Often	Sometimes	Never
Definition of business negotiation			
Business negotiation approaches			
Elements of business negotiation			
Business negotiation case study			
Process of negotiation			
Tactics of business negotiation			

 Pair work: Compare your answers with a partner.

I have never participated in business negotiation. What about you?

······ Part II　Performing ······

Reading

 New Words and Phrases

acknowledgement [əkˈnɒlɪdʒmənt] *n.* 回单；承认，确认；致谢

arbitrage rate 套汇汇率

acceptance fee 认付费

acceptance house 期票承兑行

acceptor for honor 参加承兑人

accepting bank 承兑银行

account sales 销货账，销货清单

account of goods sold 销货账目

account of receipts and payments 收支账目

accounting statement 会计报表

accounting unit 会计单位

accrued expense 应计费用

accrued item 应计项目

accumulation of capital 资本积累

acknowledgement of orders 订单确认

active demand 畅销

actual cost 实际成本

actual price 实际价

additional expense 追加费用

additional order 追加订货

additional premium 追加保费

advance in price 涨价

advance payment 预付款

advance settlement of exchange 预交外汇

🐾 Group work：Read the following sentences and learn how to use them freely.

1. Would anyone like something to drink before we begin?
   在我们正式开始前，大家喝点什么？

2. We are ready.　我们准备好了。

3. I know I can count on you.　我知道我可以相信你。

4. Trust me.　请相信我。

5. We are here to solve problems.　我们是来解决问题的。

6. I hope this meeting is productive.　我希望这是一次富有成效的会谈。

7. I need more information.　我需要更多的信息。

8. Not in the long run.　从长远来说并不是这样。

9. Let me explain to you why.　让我给你解释一下原因。

10. That's the basic problem.　这是最基本的问题。

11. Let's compromise.　我们还是各退一步吧。

12. It depends on what you want.　那要视贵方的需要而定。

13. The longer we wait，the less likely it is we will come up with anything.
    时间拖得越久，我们成功的机会就越小。

14. Is this negotiable? 还有商量的余地吗？

15. I'm sure there is some room for negotiation. 我肯定还有商量的余地。

16. We have another plan. 我们还有一个计划。

17. Let's negotiate the price. 让我们来讨论一下价格吧。

18. We could add it to the agenda. 我们可以把它列入议程。

19. Thanks for reminding us. 谢谢你提醒我们。

Listening

 Useful Expressions

covered everything in the contract 合同中涉及的一切

detailed issue 详细的问题   make an agreement on 达成协议

make a conclusion 得出结论   training program 训练方案

project assistant 项目助理   without brake 没有刹车

as for the other issues 至于其他的问题   Summer Palace 颐和园

Empress Dowager 皇太后   get bogged down 深陷泥潭；陷入困境

on details 详细地   wind up 上紧发条；使结束；收尾

Pair work：Listen to the dialogues and fill in the blanks.

音频 17－1

━━━ Dialogue 1 ━━━

Negotiation

A: I think we have _____ everything in the _____. That brings us to the final part of the _____. Miss Pan，would you like a _____ about detailed issues we have _____?

B: Yes. As talked about before，we have made an _____ on the price，_____ and the _____ of the project. But clearly，we haven't made a _____ on the _____ ____ beginning _____ and the _____ of employees that would be able to take part in the _____.

A: Oh，that could be sure as the training begins. We may leave it to the _____.

B: It's OK. Now we may make a conclusion about the contract.

A: Through the former meeting，we made _____ the price of the training program and the specific _____ of the training that includes the _____ as well as the _____ ____. The whole length of the training is seven days without _____. Is there anything you want to add?

B: As for the other _____ , I suggest we'd better leave it to the next meeting.

A: That would be OK，and I'm really sorry that I have to go now. May we stop at here?

B: No problem，and I think we all agree that we have had a _____ meeting.

A: It _____ for me to thank you for coming and my assistant will _____ taxi for you. See you next meeting.

B: It's very nice of you _____ . See you next time.

━━━━━ Dialogue 2 ━━━━━

Arranging Visit Schedule

Sun: It's a _____ to meet you，Mr. Duu.

Duu: Glad to meet you too.

音频 17 - 2

Sun: We have come to _____ that your stay in Beijing is a pleasant one.

Duu: Thank you. You're going out of your _____ for us，I believe.

Sun: Not at all. After all，it's your _____ here and we'd like you to feel _____ _____ . If there's anything _____ you can always tell us.

Duu: Thank you. The room service here is quite _____ and we like the _____ .

Sun: I'm glad you find the hotel service _____ .

Duu: Yes，I do. Were you thinking of any _____ place you wanted to take us to?

Sun: Well，we had the _____ in mind.

Duu: The summer residence of the _____ ? That would be nice. I've heard so much about it. _____ it.

Sun: Well，so long as we know what each other's _____ are and we don't get bogged down _____ . I'm sure the talks will _____ as planned.

Duu: Well，for our part，we'll do our best to make everything _____ sailing.

Sun: Thank you. If all goes well，we'll be able to _____ our talks the day after tomorrow.

Duu: I hope so. Anyway we'll _____ .

······ Part III   Practicing ······

Reading

━━━━━ New Words and Phrases ━━━━━

outcome ['aʊtkʌm] *n.* 结果；成果；出路

bargain ['bɑːgən] *n.* 交易；契约，协定

individual [ˌɪndɪ'vɪdʒuəl] *adj.* 个人的；个别的；独特的

collective [kə'lektɪv] *adj.* 集体的；共同的；集合的；集体主义的

craft [krɑːft] *n.* 手艺；船；飞行器；诡计；*v.* 手工制作；精巧地制作

transaction [træn'zækʃn] *n.* 交易，业务，事务

price [praɪs] *n.* 净价；价格，价钱；价值

amount [ə'maʊnt] *n.* 金额

dumping ['dʌmpɪŋ] *n.* 商品倾销

complementary [ˌkɒmplɪ'mentri] *adj.* 互补的；补充的，补足的

domestic business negotiation 国内商务谈判

international business negotiation 国际商务谈判；国际贸易谈判

cooperative negotiation 合作谈判

intend to 打算（做）……，想要（做）……

complementary objectives 互补的目标

total value 总值

landing charge 卸货费

customs duty 关税

stamp duty 印花税

price including mission 含佣价

port dues 港口税

return mission 回佣

port of shipment 装运港

export credit 出口信贷

export subsidy 出口津贴

exchange dumping 外汇倾销

special preference 优惠关税

bonded warehouse 保税仓库

favorable balance of trade 贸易顺差

unfavorable balance of trade 贸易逆差

import quota 进口配额制

free trade zone 自由贸易区

value of foreign trade 对外贸易值

value of international trade 国际贸易值

generalized system 普遍优惠制

port of discharge 卸货港

wholesale price 批发价

Work individually：Read the following passage and then paraphrase.

Business Negotiation

What's the definition of negotiation? Negotiation is a dialogue between two or more people or parties，intended to reach an understanding，resolve the point of difference，or gain advantage in outcome of dialogue，to produce an agreement upon courses of action，to bargain for individual or collective advantage，to craft outcomes to satisfy various interests of two or more people/parties involved in a negotiation.

Then what is business negotiation? Business negotiation is a give-and-take trading process in which the trading parties discuss the conditions of a transaction and reach an agreement. Business negotiation is a basic means of getting what you want from others，in which an agreement is reached when you and the other side have some interests that are shared and other that are opposed. Business negotiation is the process of bargaining over a set of issues for the purpose of reaching an agreement.

There are three elements of business negotiation：negotiation parties，negotiation aims and agreement. We all know that business negotiation includes domestic business negotiation and international business negotiation. I want to emphasis two approaches in negotiation. In competitive negotiation situation, the seller asks for one price, usually above the price the buyer is willing to pay. The buyer responds by offering a price below the asked price until a compromise is reached. However, the other approach means that people should sit down and share their true interests instead of focusing on their positions. Searching for common ground and being creative will result in a negotiated agreement and a much richer relationship. It is called cooperative negotiation.

The characteristics of business negotiation:

1. Negotiation is a process of information exchange between two sides.
2. Negotiation is at the heart of every transaction and for the most part, it comes down to the interaction between two sides with a common goal but divergent methods.
3. Negotiation must be to the satisfaction of both parties. It can be a very trying process with confrontation and concession.
4. Both parties share open information. They intend to find something in common.
5. Both sides try to understand each other's point of view.
6. Both parties know that they have common and conflicting objectives, so they try to find a way to achieve common and complementary objectives acceptable to them both.

Speaking

==== New Words and Phrases ====

confront [kən'frʌnt] v. 使面对

compensate ['kɒmpenseɪt] v. 补偿，偿还

arbitration [ˌɑːbɪ'treɪʃn] n. 仲裁，公断

alternative [ɔːl'tɜːnətɪv] n. 其他选择

consensus [kən'sensəs] n. 共识

cooperation [kəʊˌɒpə'reɪʃn] n. 合作

counterattack ['kaʊntərə'tæk] n. 反击

counterpart ['kaʊntəpɑːt] n. 对方

cordially ['kɔːdɪəli] adj. 诚挚的

deadlock ['dedlɒk] n. 僵局

dispute [dɪ'spjuːt] v. 争论

dominate ['dɒmɪneɪt] v. 支配，主导

entitled [ɪn'taɪtld] adj. 应得的，有资格的

hostility [hɒ'stɪləti] n. 敌意

impulse ['ɪmpʌls] n. 冲动

indecisive [ˌɪndɪ'saɪsɪv] adj. 优柔寡断的

mutual ['mjuːtʃuəl] adj. 互相的

proposal [prə'pəʊzl] n. 提案

resentment [rɪ'zentmənt] n. 积怨

tactics ['tæktɪks] n. 手段，策略

unrealistic [ˌʌnrɪə'lɪstɪk] adj. 不现实的

counter proposal 反提案

trade-off 条件交换

apply for information 探询消息

apply for remittance 托汇

appointed store 指定商店

alter an agreement 改变契约

amicable allowance 友好让价

amicable settlement 友好解决

make up for a loss 补偿，偿还

conflict resolution 冲突解决

Pair work：Listen to the dialogues and have a role play.

Dialogue 1

Price Discussion（1）

音频 17‑3

Duu: I'm glad to have the opportunity of visiting your corporation. I hope we can do business together.

Sun: It's a great pleasure to meet you, Mr. Duu. I believe you have seen our exhibits in the show room. What is it in particular you're interested in?

Duu: I'm interested in the sensor tap of the model C721B. I've seen the exhibits and studied your catalogues. I think some of the items will find a ready market in France. Here's a list of requirements. I'd like to have your lowest quotations.

Sun: Thank you for your inquiry. Would you tell us what quantity you require so that we can work out the offers.

Duu: I'll do that. Meanwhile, could you give me an indication of the price?

Sun: Here are our CIF price. All the prices in the lists are subject to our confirmation.

Duu: What about the commission? From European suppliers I usually get a 3 to 5 percent commission for my imports. It's the general practice.

Sun: As a rule we do not allow any commission. But if the order is a sizable one, we'll consider it.

Duu: You see, I do business on a commission basis. A commission on your price would make it easier for me to promote sales. Even 2 or 3 percent would help.

Sun: We'll discuss this when you place your order with us. When shall I hear from you?

Duu: OK. Next Friday.

Dialogue 2

Price Discussion（2）

音频 17‑4

Duu: I've come about your offer for bristles. We intend to 1,000 dozen sensor taps.

Sun: I have here our price sheet on an FOB basis. The prices are given without engagement.

Duu: Good. If you excuse me, I'll go over the sheet right now.

Sun: Take your time, please.

Duu: I can tell you at a glance that your prices are much too high.

Sun: This is our rock-bottom price, Mr. Duu. We can't make any further concessions.

Duu: If that's the case, there's not much point in further discussion. We might as well call the whole deal off.

Sun: What I mean is that we'll never be able to come down to your price. The gap is too great.

Duu: I think it is unwise for either of us to insist on his own price. How about meeting each other half way and each makes a further concession so that the business can be conclu-ded?

Sun: What is your proposal?

Duu: Your unit price is 100 dollars higher than we can accept. When I suggested we meet each other half way, I meant it literally.

Sun: Do you mean to suggest that we have to make a further reduction of 50 dollars in our price? That's impossible!

Duu: What would you suggest?

Sun: The best we can do will be a reduction of another 30 dollars. That'll definitely be rock bottom.

Duu: That still leaves a gap of 20 dollars to be covered. Let's meet each other half way once more, then the gap will be closed and our business completed.

Sun: You certainly have a way of talking me into it. All right. Let's meet half way again. OK, USD 60 per FOB Dalian, 1,000 dozen in total.

Duu: I'm glad we've come to an agreement on price.

Unit 18 Business Contract

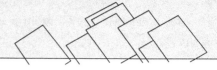

In this unit, the students are required to grasp the following contents.

1. Learning to talk something about business contract with some given useful words and phrases of this unit freely.
2. Learning to talk something about business contract with some given useful sentences of this unit freely.
3. Reading a passage about business contract and then paraphrasing it.
4. Listening and having a role play.

······ Part I Preparing ······

 Work individually: What contents does business contract include?

About business contract	Often	Sometimes	Never
Definition of business contract			
Titles or names and domiciles of the parties			
Target, quality and quantity			
Price or remuneration			
Time limit, place and method of performance			
Liability for breach of a contract			
Method of dispute resolution			

 Pair work: Compare your answers with a partner.

Do you know anything about business contract?

······· Part II　Performing ·······

Reading

New Words and Phrases

hover ['hɒvə(r)] *v.* 徘徊于……，盘旋于

moderately ['mɒdərətli] *adv.* 适当地，合适地；适度

utmost ['ʌtməʊst] *n.* 极限，竭尽所能

economically [ˌiːkə'nɒmɪkli] *adv.* 经济地，便宜地

ceiling price 最高价，顶价

Group work：Read the following sentences and learn how to use them freely.

1. The contract for the contractual joint venture shall continue from a period of two years thereafter.
本合作经营企业合同此后应持续有效两年。

2. The buyer hereby orders from the seller the under mentioned goods subject to the following.
买方向卖方订购下列商品，条件如下。

3. For purpose of this, capital account shall be adjusted hypothetically as provided for in Section 4. 6 herein.
基于此，应依照本合同第四条第六款调整资金账户。

4. The buyer shall nevertheless have the right to cancel in part or in whole of the contract without prejudice to the buyer's right to claim compensations.
在不妨碍买方索赔权的情况下，买方仍有权取消合同的部分或全部内容。

5. The contract comes into effect today, and we can't go back on our word now.
合同已于今日生效，我们不能反悔了。

6. Once the contract is approved by the Chinese government, it is legally binding upon both parties.
合同一经中国政府批准，对双方就有了法律约束力。

7. We have to hold you to the contract.
我们不得不要求你们按合同办事。

8. There is an arbitration clause in the contract. (or insurance clause, inspection clause, shipping clause...)
合同中有一项仲裁条款。（或：保险条款、检验条款、装运条款等）

9. We sincerely hope that both quality and quantity are in conformity with the contract stipulations.
我们真诚希望质量、数量都与合同规定相吻合。

10. The contract states that the supplier will be charged a penalty if there is a delay in delivery.
合同规定如果供货商延误交货期，将被罚款。

11. These are two originals of the contract we prepared.

这是我们准备好的两份合同正本。

12. We always carry out the terms of our contract to the letter and stand by what we say.

我们坚持重合同、守信用。

13. You have no grounds for backing out of the contract.

你们没有正当理由背弃合同。

14. In case one party fails to carry out the contract, the other party is entitled to cancel the contract.

如果一方不执行合同，另一方有权撤销该合同。

15. We offered a much lower price, so they got the contract.

由于我们报价更低，他们和我们签了合同。

16. Are you worrying about the non-execution of the contract and non-payment on our part?

你是否担心我们不履行合同或者拒不付款？

17. You cannot cancel the contract without first securing our agreement.

如果没有事先征得我们同意，你们不能取消合同。

18. We signed a contract for medicines. 我们签订了一份药品合同。

19. A Japanese company and SINOCHEM have entered into a new contract.

中国中化集团有限公司已经和日本一家公司签订了一份新合同。

20. I know we (the seller) should draw up a contract and the buyer has to sign it.

我们知道我们（卖方）应该拟出一份合同，买方必须签署合同。

Listening 🎧

══ Useful Expressions ══

sign a sales contract 签订一份销售合同　　reach agreement on 就……达成一致

all the terms 一切条款　　have an agreement on 就……达成一致

look... over 看一看　　in the shape 顺利，健康

in the shape of 以……形状，通过……方式　on the bottom 在下面

nice to be finished 结果让人十分满意　　draft of contract 合同草案

long and stable business relations 长期稳定的业务关系

at least three years 至少三年　　nothing more 没有了

reach a basic agreement on 就……基本达成协议

make a great effort 做出很大努力　　two formal copies of the contract 两份合同

bear fruit 结出硕果　　in no time 立即，马上

continue cooperation 继续合作

further extension of trade relations 贸易关系的进一步发展

音频 18-1

 Pair work：Listen to the dialogues and fill in the blanks.

━━━━ Dialogue 1 ━━━━

Signing a Sales Contract（1）

A: Mr. Wang，we have reached _____ on all the terms. Now we should sign _____，I think.

B: I'm very glad we have an _____ on this particular _____. Here is the contract.

A: I'd like to look this over before I _____ it.

B: Of course. Please _____ and see if it contains all we have _____ on during our _____.

A: It looks fine to me. Everything is _____.

B: Just sign there on the _____. Here's a pen.

A: Thank you. Where do you want me to _____?

B: Right here.

A: How's that?

B: That's _____.

A: Here's my _____.

B: And mine. Here's your _____ of the contract.

A: Good. I'm glad we're all done.

B: Yes，it's nice to be _____. I hope this _____ the beginning of _____ and _____ business relations between us. Let's go out and _____.

A: I think we both need a _____.

━━━━ Dialogue 2 ━━━━

Signing a Sales Contract（2）

音频 18-2

Tom: We've brought the _____ of our contract. Please have a look.

Mike: How long will the _____ last?

Tom: This contract is _____ for one year.

Mike: I'm afraid that one year is too _____. This contract must be valid for _____ three years.

Tom: If everything's _____ satisfactorily，it could be _____ for two years.

Mike: All right. We _____ your suggestion.

Tom: What do you think of the _____?

139

Mike: The wording is really idiomatic. I'm very _____ with it.

Tom: Is there any other _____?

Mike: No. _____.

Tom: We have finally reached a basic _____ on the problems that should be _____.

Mike: Both of our parties have made a great _____.

Tom: That's true. It is time for us to sign the _____.

Mike: I've been looking forward to this _____.

Tom: Now, please _____ it.

Mike: Done. Congratulations.

Tom: Each of us has two formal copies of the _____, one in Chinese and one in English. Would you _____ these two copies?

Mike: Thank you very much. I think the _____ will bear fruit in no time, and I hope our continuing _____ and further extension of our _____.

Tom: That's what I want, too. Let me _____ a toast to the _____ of our negotiations, and to our future _____, cheers!

Mike: Cheers!

• • • • • • Part III   Practicing • • • • • •

Reading

▰▰▰▰ New Words and Phrases ▰▰▰▰

contradict [ˌkɒntrəˈdɪkt] *v.* 反驳，驳斥；否认

initiator [ɪˈnɪʃɪeɪtə(r)] *n.* 发起人；创始人

offerer [ˈɒfərə] *n.* 发盘人；〈经〉发价人

offeree [ˌɒfərˈiː] *n.* 被发价人，受盘人

lease [liːs] *n.* 租约；租契；租赁物；租赁权

bolster [ˈbəʊlstə(r)] *v.* 支持；支撑；鼓励

terminate [ˈtɜːmɪneɪt] *v.* 结束；使终结；解雇

attorney [əˈtɜːni] *n.* 律师；代理人

refer to 参考；指的是；涉及；适用于

parole contracts 假释的合同

unsealed written contract 密封的书面合同

an oral contract 口头合同

in written form 书面形式；书面

elementary banking 中小银行

an informal business contract 非正式的商务合同

a legal contract 法律合同

binds... into 把……结合至……

a mutual agreement 共同的协议

negotiated terms and conditions 协议的条款和条件

lease specialized equipment 租赁专业设备

original offer [法] 原要约，原提议，原发价

multiple rounds of amendments and negotiations 多轮修正和谈判

a binding agreement 有约束力的协议

price and payment terms 价格和付款条件

claim outstanding payments 索赔未支付

bolster one's position 支持……的位置

in a dispute 在争议中

a written record of the agreement 协议的书面记录

commercial construction projects 商业建设项目

regardless of scope 不论范围

cancel a construction contract with his general contractor 取消他的总承包施工合同

 Work individually：Read the following passage and then paraphrase.

What is an Informal Business Contract?

An informal business contact can refer to either an oral contract or all contracts that are not under seal or of record. These are also called parole contracts. Usually, an unsealed written contract is considered more binding as compared to an oral contract. The agreements in written form cannot be contradicted.

Process

According to elementary banking, an informal business contract does not require any witness nor does it require a seal. The wording of the contract should be simple and brief and should not contain any confusing statements. It should fully state the intentions of both parties.

Oral Contract

It is hard to prove an agreement based on oral contract only. It is always beneficial to put the oral contract into an informal written contract that is signed by both parties.

What Three Elements Are Necessary for a Legal Contract?

A legal contract binds two or more parties into a mutual agreement based on negotiated terms and conditions. In order for contracts to be considered legal, three specific elements must always be present. These elements are required in all contracts, oral or written.

the Offer

For a contract to be binding, the first element that must be present is an offer. The initiator of the contract, known as the offerer, presents a proposal that outlines what types of services or goods will be provided to the offeree. The offeree is the party that accepts the offer and joins into the agreement. An example of a services-related offer is that of a hospital contracting with a specialist doctor to provide professional services. For a goods-related offer, a hospital might contract with a medical manufacturer to lease specialized equipment.

the Acceptance

The acceptance is the second part of the contract that must be present. Here, one party accepts the terms of the contract as presented by the other party. In order for acceptance to take place, both parties must agree on all conditions of the contract. If the offeree proposes changes to the original offer, for instance, the contract must be renegotiated until both parties agree on the terms. It is possible for contracts to go through multiple rounds of amendments and negotiations until the offer is accepted.

the Consideration

The consideration is the final part of the contract that must be present. Consideration sets out what will be exchanged between the offerer and the offeree, such as whether they are exchanging goods for money, services for money, goods for goods or services for services. This element is essential for establishing a binding agreement regarding price and payment terms. Each party in the contract has to know what he is responsible for doing and what he will get in exchange.

Signatures

While oral contracts can be legally binding, having a signed contract with both parties' signatures is good for both recordkeeping and peace of mind. If you ever need to provide evidence of your contract, such as to claim outstanding payments or bolster your position in a dispute, it helps to have a written record of the agreement.

How to Terminate a General Contractor Contract

Commercial construction projects, regardless of scope, often experience delay or other problems. At times, these problems may cause the owner of a business to cancel a construction contract with his general contractor. Because commercial construction projects are usually governed by a written contract, the written contract forms the basis for determining whether a business owner can terminate that contract, and under what conditions. Most contracts also address the issue of what payments or damages a general contractor might be owed upon termination of the contract. Business owners should contact an attorney to help assess liability prior to terminating a contract with a general contractor.

Speaking

——— New Words and Phrases ———

catalogue ['kætəlɒg] *n.* 目录

accept [ək'sept] *v.* 接受

acceptance [ək'septəns] *n.* 接受

acceptable [ək'septəbl] *adj.* 可接受的；合意的

unit price 单价

price list 价目表

terms of contract 契约条款

sign a contract 签合同

check terms 商定条款

with pleasure 非常愿意

the most favorable price 最优惠的价格

the best discount 最大的折扣

make delivery 交货

delivery spread 分批交货

a period of time 一段时间

Pair work: Listen to the dialogues and have a role play.

音频 18 - 3

============ Dialogue 1 ============

Signing a Contract

A: Can you tell me what the unit price of such carpet is?

B: Of course. Here is the catalogue and the price list. You can have a look. We also have many other kinds of carpets.

A: The price seems acceptable for me. But I want to check whether you can supply the carpet now if we order some?

B: Of course we can. We can provide the quantity you ask for.

A: That's very good. Shall we sign a contract now?

B: No problem. Let's check the terms of contract.

============ Dialogue 2 ============

Checking Terms

音频 18 - 4

A: We'd like to buy 2000 tons of rice from your company. Can you give me an indication of your prices?

B: With pleasure. You'll find that we have given you the most favorable price in our business.

A: OK，let me have a look. We shall be glad if you will quote us the best discount for cash off your list price for cash for this quantity.

B: Please feel assured that we will give you the best discount we can give.

A: Thank you very much. I also want to know how long it will take to make delivery.

B: Three months. Would you accept delivery spread over a period of time?

A: Yes，we normally do.

Unit 19 International Payment

▬▬▬ Objectives ▬▬▬

In this unit, the students are required to grasp the following contents.

1. Learning to talk something about international payment with some given useful words and phrases of this unit freely.

2. Learning to talk something about international payment with some given useful sentences of this unit freely.

3. Reading a passage about international payment and then paraphrasing it.

4. Listening and having a role play about international payment.

······ **Part I Preparing** ······

 Work individually: What contents does international payment include?

About international payment	Often	Sometimes	Never
Words of "Bill of Exchange" or "Draft"			
Date and place of issuance of draft			
A specific sum which shall be exactly the same with that indicated on export invoice			
Name of the drawee			
Name and signature of the drawer			
Name of the payee or order or bearer			
Endorsement of the payee when applicable			

 Pair work: Compare your answers with a partner.

Do you know anything about international payment?

······ Part II   Performing ······

Reading

New Words and Phrases

dishonour [dɪsˈɒnə(r)] *n.* 拒付

discount [ˈdɪskaʊnt] *n.* 贴现

cheque [tʃek] *n.* 支票

invoice [ˈɪnvɔɪs] *n.* 发票

remittance [rɪˈmɪtns] *n.* 汇付

collection [kəˈlekʃn] *n.* 托收

copy [ˈkɒpi] *n.* 副本

original [əˈrɪdʒənl] *n.* 正本

dealing [ˈdiːlɪŋ] *n.* 交易，生意

stage [steɪdʒ] *n.* 阶段，过程

destination [ˌdestɪˈneɪʃn] *n.* 目的地

beneficiary [ˌbenɪˈfɪʃəri] *n.* 受益人

guarantor [ˌɡærənˈtɔː(r)] *n.* 保证人

bearer [ˈbeərə(r)] *n.* 持票人

payer [ˈpeɪə(r)] *n.* 付款人

consignee [ˈkɒnsaɪˈniː] *n.* 受托人

consignor [kənˈsaɪnə] *n.* 委托人

principal [ˈprɪnsəpl] *n.* 委托人

truster [ˈtrʌstə] *n.* 信托人

acceptor [əkˈseptə] *n.* 承兑人

trustee [trʌˈstiː] *n.* 被信托人

endorser [ɪnˈdɔːsə] *n.* 背书人

endorsee [ˌɪndɔːˈsiː] *n.* 被背书人

endorse [ɪnˈdɔːs] *n.* 背书

holder [ˈhəʊldə(r)] *n.* 持票人

endorsement [ɪnˈdɔːsmənt] *n.* 背书

bailee [beɪˈliː] *n.* 受托人，代保管人

deferred payment 延期付款

progressive payment 分期付款

payment on terms 定期付款

payment agreement 支付协定

pay order 支付凭证

payment order 付款通知

payment by banker 银行支付

payment by remittance 汇拨支付

payment in part 部分付款

payment in full 全部付讫

clean payment 单纯支付

simple payment 单纯支付

payment by installment 分期付款

payment respite 延期付款

payment at maturity 到期付款

payment in advance 预付（货款）

cash with order（C. W. O）随订单付现

cash on delivery（C. O. D）交货付现

cash against documents（C. A. D）凭单付现

pay on delivery（P. O. D）货到付款

payment in kind 实物支付

payment for（in）cash 现金支付，付现

payment terms 支付条件，付款方式

the mode of payment 付款方式

documentary bill 跟单汇票

sight bill 即期汇票

time bill 远期汇票

usance bill 远期汇票

commercial bill 商业汇票

banker's bill 银行汇票

commercial acceptance bill 商业承兑汇票

bankers' acceptance bill 银行承兑汇票

sample invoice 样品发票

consignment invoice 寄售发票

recipe invoice 收妥发票

certified invoice 证明发票

manufacturers' invoice 厂商发票

at sight 即期，见票即付

mail transfer（M/T）信汇

demand draft（D/D）票汇

telegraphic transfer（T/T）电汇

clean bill for collection 光票托收

documentary bill for collection 跟单托收

uniform rules for collection 托收统一规则

collection advice 托收委托书

advice of clean bill for collection 光票托收委托书

collection bill purchased 托收出口押汇

trust receipt 信托收据

documents against payment（D/P）付款交单

documents against payment at sight（D/P sight）即期付款交单

documents against payment after sight（D/P sight）远期付款交单

documents against acceptance（D/A）承兑交单

cash against payment 凭单付款

letter of credit（L/C）信用证

form of credit 信用证形式

terms of validity 信用证效期

expiry date 效期

date of issue 开证日期

L/C amount 信用证金额

L/C number 信用证号码

open by airmail 信开

open by cable 电开

open by brief cable 简电开证

amend L/C 修改信用证

fixed L/C or fixed amount L/C 有固定金额的信用证

sight L/C 即期信用证

usance L/C 远期信用证

buyer's usance L/C 买方远期信用证

traveler's L/C 旅行信用证

revocable L/C 可撤销的信用证

irrevocable L/C 不可撤销的信用证

confirmed L/C 保兑的信用证

unconfirmed L/C 不保兑的信用证

confirmed Irrevocable L/C 保兑的不可撤销信用证

irrevocable unconfirmed L/C 不可撤销不保兑的信用证

transferable L/C 可转让信用证

untransferable L/C 不可转让信用证

revolving L/C 循环信用证

reciprocal L/C 对开信用证

back to back L/C 背对背信用证

countervailing credit（俗称）子证

overriding credit 母证

banker's acceptance L/C 银行承兑信用证

trade acceptance L/C 商业承兑信用证

red clause L/C 红条款信用证

anticipatory L/C 预支信用证

credit payable by a trader 商业付款信用证

credit payable by a bank 银行付款信用证

without recourse 不受追索

exporter's bank 出口方银行

importer's bank 进口方银行

seller's bank 卖方银行

buyer's bank 买方银行

paying bank 付款行，汇入行

remitting bank 汇出行

opening bank 开证行

issuing bank 开证行

advising bank 通知行

notifying bank 通知行

negotiating bank 议付行

drawee bank 付款行

confirming bank 保兑行

presenting bank 提示行

transmitting bank 转递行

accepting bank 承兑行

payment against documents 凭单付款

payment against documents through collection
　凭单托收付款

payment by acceptance 承兑付款

payment by bill 凭汇票付款

letter of guarantee（L/G）保证书

bank guarantee 银行保函

contract guarantee 合约保函

payment guarantee 付款保证书

repayment guarantee 还款保证书

import guarantee 进口保证书

tender/bid guarantee 投标保证书

performance guarantee 履约保证书

retention money guarantee 保留金保证书

documents of title to the goods 物权凭证

authority to purchase（A/P）委托购买证

letter of indication 印鉴核对卡

letter of hypothecation 质押书

general letter of hypothecation 总质押书

 Group work： Read the following sentences and learn how to use them freely.

1. The buyer suggested D/A as the terms of payment，but the seller was unwilling to make any exception. 买方建议用承兑交单作为付款方式，但卖方不愿例外。

2. We can't agree to draw at 30 days D/A. 我们不同意开具 30 天期的承兑交单汇票。

3. So it's better for us to adopt D/P or D/A. 因此，最好是采用付款交单方式或承兑交单方式。

4. I suppose D/P or D/A should be adopted as the mode of payment this time.
  我建议这次用付款交单或承兑交单方式来付款。

5. It would help me greatly if you would accept D/A or D/P.
  如果您能接受 D/A 或 D/P 付款，那可帮了我们大忙。

6. Could you make an exception and accept D/A or D/P?
  您能否破个例，接受 D/A 或 D/P 付款方式？

7. We insist on a letter of credit. 我们坚持用信用证方式付款。

8. As I've said，we require payment by L/C. 我已经说过了，我们要求以信用证付款。

9. We still intend to use letter of credit as the term of payment.
  我们仍然想用信用证付款方式。

10. We always require L/C for our exports. 我们出口一向要求以信用证付款。

11. L/C at sight is normal for our exports to France.
  我们向法国出口一般使用即期信用证付款。

12. We pay by L/C for our imports. 进口我们也采用信用证汇款。

13. Our terms of payment is confirmed and irrevocable letter of credit.
  我们的付款条件是保兑的不可撤销的信用证。

14. You must be aware that an irrevocable L/C gives the exporter the additional protection of banker's guarantee.

你必须意识到不可撤销信用证为出口商提供了银行担保。

15. Is the wording of "confirmed" necessary for the letter of credit?

信用证上还用写明"保兑"字样吗?

16. For payment we require 100% value, irrevocable L/C in our favour with partial shipment allowed clause available by draft at sight.

我们要求用不可撤销的、允许分批装运、金额为全部货款,并以我方为抬头人的信用证,凭即期汇票支付。

17. What do you say to 50% by L/C and the balance by D/P?

50%用信用证,其余的用付款交单,您看怎么样?

18. Please notify us of L/C number by telex immediately.

请立即电传通知我方信用证号码。

19. Will you please increase the credit to ＄1000? 能不能把信用证金额增至 1000 美元?

Listening 🎧

━━━━ **Useful Expressions** ━━━━

mode of payment 付款方式   a deferred payment 延期付款

pay off 付清   sign the agreement 签署协议

in connection with 和……有关   make payment 付款

business friends 商界朋友   Japan currency 日元

the National Westminster Bank and Barclays Bank

国民西敏寺银行和巴克莱银行

sales confirmation or contract 销售确认书或合同

 Pair work: Listen to the dialogues and fill in the blanks.

━━━━ Dialogue 1 ━━━━

音频 19-1

International Payment (1)

A: Mr. Wang, we haven't discussed the mode of _____.

B: You know, Mr. Forster, this is a really large purchase. I'm _____ we can't pay off at one time. We have to pay by _____.

A: Do you mean you _____ a deferred payment?

B: Yes, Mr. Forster.

A: When do you _____ the payment then?

B: We'll start our payment in half a year and the total _____ will be paid off within 2 years by three installments（分期付款）.

A: We can accept that，but you have to pay the _____.

B: All right.

A: Shall we sign the _____ now?

B: OK，let's _____ it.

━━━━━ Dialogue 2 ━━━━━

International Payment（2）

音频 19‐2

Black: Well，Mr. White，we've settled everything in _____ with this transaction except the _____ of payment in yen. Now can you _____ to me how to make payment in yen?

White: Many of our _____ friends in England，France，Switzerland，Italy and Germany are _____ for our exports in Japan _____. It is quite easy to do so.

Black: I know some of them are doing that. But this is new to me. I've never _____ payment in yen before. It is _____ to make payment in _____ sterling，but I may have some _____ in making payment in yen.

White: Many banks in Europe now carry _____ in yen. They are in a _____ to open letters of credit and effect payment in yen. Consult your _____ and you'll see that they are _____ to offer you this _____.

Black: Do you mean to say that I can open a letter of _____ in yen with a _____ in London or Bonn?

White: Sure you can. Several of the banks in London，such as the _____ Westminster Bank and Barclays Bank are in a position to _____ letters of credit in yen. They'll do so _____ our sales confirmation or _____.

Black: I see.

········ **Part III　Practicing** ········

Reading

━━━━━ New Words and Phrases ━━━━━

domestic [dəˈmestɪk] *adj.* 国内的　　　　sound [saʊnd] *adj.* 健全的；良好的

invoice ['ɪnvɔɪs] *n.* 发票	periodic payments 分阶段付款
status ['steɪtəs] *n.* 状况	usance draft (tenor draft, term draft)
remittance [rɪ'mɪtns] *n.* 汇款	远期汇票
debtor ['detə(r)] *n.* 债务人	documentary draft 跟单汇票
debit ['debɪt] *v.* 将……记入借方 *n.* 借方;	clean draft 光票
记入借方的款	bill of lading 提单
default [dɪ'fɔːlt] *n.* 违约；不履行职责	title of the goods 货物所有权
ban [bæn] *v.* /*n.* 禁止	insurance policy 保险单
fluctuation ['flʌktʃʊ'eɪʃn] *n.* 波动	documentary collection 跟单托收
hesitant ['hezɪtənt] *adj.* 犹豫的；不情愿的	documents against payment (D/P) 付款交单
dubious ['djuːbɪəs] *adj.* 可疑的	documents against acceptance (D/A) 承兑交单
draft [drɑːft] *n.* 汇票	with discretion 慎重地；审慎地
bill of exchange 汇票	
credit worthiness 资信可靠状况	

 Work individually：Read the following passage and then paraphrase.

International Payment

Generally speaking, it is not very difficult for buyers and sellers in domestic trade to get to know each other's financial status and other information, and payment is likely to be made in a straight forward manner, say by remittance or by debiting the debtor's account. In international trade, however, things are far more complicated. Purchase and sale of goods and services are carried out beyond national boundaries, which makes it rather difficult for the parties concerned in the transaction to get adequate information about each other's financial standing and credit worthiness. Therefore, mutual trust is hard to build. Both the exporter and the importer face risks as there is always the possibility that the other party may not fulfill the contract.

For the exporter there is the risk of buyer default. The importer might fail to pay in full for the goods. He might go bankrupt ; his government might, for various reasons, ban trade with the exporting country or ban imports of certain commodities; the buyer might run into difficulties getting the foreign exchange to pay for the goods. It is even possible that the buyer is not reliable and simply refuses to pay the agreed amount on various excuses.

On the part of the importer, there is the risk that the shipment will be delayed, and he might only receive them long after payment. The delay may be caused by problems in production or transportation, and such delays may lead to loss of business. There is also a risk that wrong goods might be sent as a result of negligence of the exporter because of his lack of integrity.

Polities risks such as war, quotas, foreign exchange control; commercial risks like market change and exchange rate fluctuations; and even language barriers all add up to the problems in international trade. Because of these problems and risks, exporters are hesitant to release their goods before receiving payment, while importers prefer to have control over the goods before parting with their money. Various methods of payment have been developed to cope with different situations in international trade. When the political and economic situation in the importing country makes payment uncertain or when the buyer's credit standing is dubious, the exporter may prefer cash in advance or partial cash in advance. In this case, the importer has no guarantee that the exporter will fulfill his obligations once he has made payment by cash. If the buyer and the seller know each other well, they may decide to trade on open account. This means that no documents are involved and that legally the buyer can pay anytime. The seller loses all control over the goods once they have been shipped. Sales on this basis are usually paid for by periodic payments, and obviously the exporter must have sufficient financial strength to carry the cost of the goods' until receiving payment. If the exporter wishes to retain title or ownership to the goods, he can enter into consignment transactions. This means the exporter has to send his goods abroad and will not get payment until the goods are sold. If not sold, the goods can be shipped back. Therefore, this arrangement should only be made with full understanding of the risks involved and is preferably to be limited to stable countries where the exporter has a trusted agent to look after his interest.

A lot of international transactions are paid for by means of the draft, which, also referred to as the bill of exchange, is an unconditional order to a bank or a customer to pay a sum of money to someone on demand or at a fixed time in the future. The person who draws the draft, usually the exporter, is called the drawer, and the person to whom the draft is drawn is called the drawee. There is yet another party, the payee, i. e. the person receiving the payment, who and the drawer are generally but not necessarily the same person, as the drawer can instruct the drawee either to pay "to the order of ourselves" or to the order of someone else, for instance, the bank.

A draft is either a sight draft or a usance draft (also called tenor draft or term draft). The former calls for immediate payment on presentation to the drawee while the latter is payable at a later date, e. g. 30, 45, 60, or 90 days after sight or date. A draft is either clean (without documents) or documentary. In the latter case, the draft is accompanied by the relevant documents such as the bill of lading, the invoice, the insurance policy etc.

In documentary collection, the exporter sends the draft and the shipping documents representing title to the goods to his bank, which forwards them to another bank in the importer's country, which in turn contacts the customer. In the case of documents against payment (D/P), documents will not be released to the importer until payment is effected.

There are D/P at sight and D/P after sight. The former requires immediate payment by the importer to get hold of the documents. The latter gives the importer a certain period after presentation of the documents, but documents are not released to him until he actually pays for the merchandise. In the case of documents against acceptance (D/A), documents are handed over to the importer upon his acceptance of the bill of exchange drawn by the exporter. Payment will not be made until a later date. D/A is always after sight.

So far as the exporter's interest is concerned, D/P at sight is more favorable than D/P after sight, and D/P is more favorable than D/A. In actual trade, payment by collection should be accepted with discretion. It is usually used when the financial standing of the importer is sound, or when the exporter wishes to push the sale of his goods, or when the transaction involves only a small quantity. Otherwise, the letter of credit is generally preferred.

Speaking

New Words and Phrases

sterling ['stɜːlɪŋ] n. 英国货币；标准纯银；银器

refusal [rɪ'fjuːzl] n. 拒绝；优先取舍权

decline [dɪ'klaɪn] n. 下降，下跌

commodity [kə'mɒdəti] n. 产品

convenient [kən'viːnɪənt] adj. 方便的

the refusal of payment 拒付

the bank interest 银行利息

something goes wrong 某事上出问题，出现差错

an eye to future business 考虑到以后的生意

make concessions 做出让步

technical data 技术资料

tunnel drillers 隧道钻机

Business is closed at this price. 交易就按此价敲定。

go over the other terms and conditions of the transaction 检查一下这项交易的其他条款

no objection to the stipulations about the

packing and shipping marks 同意关于包装和唛头的条款

new strong wooden cases 崭新牢固的木箱

long distance ocean transportation 长途海洋运输

against dampness, moisture, rust, and be able to stand shock and rough handling 防湿、防潮、防锈、防震，并且经得起粗鲁的搬运

inspection and claims 商检和索赔

Foreign Trade Arbitration Commission for the Promotion of International Trade 国际贸易促进会的对外贸易仲裁委员会

no occasion for arbitration 不需要仲裁

keep to the principle of equality and mutual benefit 坚持平等互利的原则

in a couple of days 几天内

That suits us fine. 太好了！

Pair work: Listen to the dialogues and have a role play.

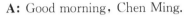 Dialogue 1

音频 19 - 3

International Payment (3)

A: Good morning，Chen Ming.

B: Good morning，Andersen.

A: Payment is to be effected (made) before the end of this month.

B: It's convenient to make payment in pound sterling.

A: Now，as regards payment，we've agreed to use U. S. dollar，am I right?

B: We may have some difficulties making payment in Japanese yen.

A: I've never made payment in Renminbi before.

B: We can't accept payment on deferred terms.

A: What's your reason for the refusal of payment?

B: Collection is not paid.

A: We don't think you'll refuse to pay.

B: Only one refusal of payment is acceptable to the bank.

A: You ought to pay us the bank interest once payment is wrongly refused.

B: We'll not pay until shipping documents for the goods have reached us.

A: We're worrying that a decline in prices might lead to refusal of payment.

B: Of course payment might be refused if anything goes wrong with the documents.

A: The equipment will be paid in installments with the commodities produced by our factory.

B: All right.

Dialogue 2

音频 19 - 4

International Payment (4)

A: Good morning，Mrs. Wang. Any news?

B: Yes. I've succeeded in persuading our export manager to agree to a reduction of ten per-cent. He made this an exception with an eye to future business.

A: Good. We certainly appreciate your making these concessions for us.

B: May I repeat 15 tunnel drillers，specifications as shown in the technical data，at 57,000 Swiss Francs each，F. O. B. European Main Ports? Business is closed at this price.

A: Yes，that's right. Shall we go over the other terms and conditions of the transaction to see if we agree on all the particulars?

B: All right. We have no objection to the stipulations about the packing and shipping marks. As a matter of fact，we always pack our machines in new strong wooden cases suitable for long distance ocean transportation.

A: The machines must be well protected against dampness, moisture, rust, and be able to stand shock and rough handling.

B: We'll see to that.

A: They are to be shipped not later than September 2001.

B: There's no question about that.

A: And what about the terms of payment?

B: Payment by L/C, to be opened by the buyer 15 to 20 days prior to the date of delivery. That's what we've agreed upon, isn't it?

A: Yes, quite so.

B: We'd like to add the condition that the letter of credit shall be valid until the 15th day after shipment. You know, it sometimes takes us a week or so to get all the shipping documents ready for the presentation and negotiation. This will give us more leeway.

A: That can be done. Any questions about the insection and claims?

B: None what so ever. The quality and performance of our machines can stand every possible test. We agree to your conditions.

A: Do you also agree to the condition that all disputes, if unsettled, shall be referred to the Foreign Trade Arbitration Commission for the Promotion of International Trade?

B: Certainly, but I'm sure there will be no occasion for arbitration.

A: Well, then, we've agreed on all the major points.

B: Yes, Mr. Brown. We're glad the deal has come off nicely and hope there will be more to come.

A: So long as we keep to the principle of equality and mutual benefit, trade between our two countries will develop further.

B: When can the contract be ready for signature?

A: I'll have it ready in a couple of days.

B: The earlier, the better. I'm leaving next week.

A: How about next Monday afternoon at 5? I'll have a copy of the contract sent to your hotel in the morning for you to look over.

B: That suits us fine.

Unit 20 Customs

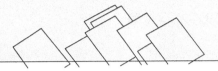

======= Objectives =======

In this unit, the students are required to grasp the following contents.

1. Learning to talk something about customs with some given useful words and phrases of this unit freely.
2. Learning to talk something about customs with some given useful sentences of this unit freely.
3. Reading a passage about customs and then paraphrasing it.
4. Listening and having a role play.

······· **Part I   Preparing** ·······

 Work individually: What contents does customs include?

About customs	Often	Sometimes	Never
An authority or agency in a country responsible for collecting tariffs and for controlling the flow of goods			
A tariff or tax			
Immigration authorities			
Domestic or international arrest warrants			
Government agreements and international laws			
Bonded store			
All authorized ports are recognized customs areas			

 Pair work: Compare your answers with a partner.

Do you know anything about customs?

•••••• Part II Performing ••••••

Reading

◼◼◼◼ New Words and Phrases ◼◼◼◼

abate [əˈbeɪt] *v.* 减轻，撤销（法令等）

assign [əˈsaɪn] *v.* 转让

confiscate [ˈkɒnfɪskeɪt] *v.* 没收

bond [bɒnd] *n.* 保税；担保

bulletin [ˈbʊlətɪn] *n.* 告示

fees [ˈfiːz] *n.* 规费

breach [briːtʃ] *n.* 违犯

bonus [ˈbəʊnəs] *n.* 津贴

conductive [kənˈdʌktɪv] *adj.* 有助于……的

credit [ˈkredɪt] *n.* 贷方

charge [tʃɑːdʒ] *n.* 收税，收费

ensure [ɪnˈʃʊə(r)] *v.* 使……必发生

fine [faɪn] *n.* 罚金；罚款

enterprise [ˈentəpraɪz] *n.* 企业单位

entrust [ɪnˈtrʌst] *v.* 委托，信托

entry [ˈentri] *n.* 报关手续；报单；进入；入口

forge [fɔːdʒ] *v.* 伪造

debit [ˈdebɪt] *n.* 借方

disburse [dɪsˈbɜːs] *v.* 支付

anti-dump 反倾销

ad valorem duty 从价税

client representative 客户代理人

compliance area 海关守法范围

a consumption entry 消费商品进口报关

a brokerage firm 报关行

consumer taste 消费税

declaration form 报关单

dutiable goods 应税货物

duty assessment office 征税部门

automated clearing house 自动化结算系统

electronic invoices 电子发票

establish the entered value 确立报关单价格

economic interests 经济利益

Electronic Data Interchange（EDI）电子数据交换

accompanying article 携带物品

enter into 与……订约；开始

accord to 给予

customs sub-office 海关分关

according to 按照

foreign trade zone 对外贸易区

consist of 由……组成

fill in 填写

final clearance 结关放行

final decision 最后决定

account for 占……比率

fixed duty 固定关税

General Customs Administration 海关总署

general deduction 一般减税

🐝 Group work：Read the following sentences and learn how to use them freely.

1. The quarantine of these objects is qualified，so you can take them away.

   这些物品经检疫合格，您可以带走了。

2. This is voucher of detaining or quarantine treatment. 这是留检/处理凭证。

3. Here're my passport and vaccination certificate. 这是我的护照和防疫证。

4. Would you please open the door of cargo bay? 请把货舱门打开好吗?

5. Could you please show your documents of approval and quarantine certificate issued by export country? 请您出示审批单和输出国检疫证书。

6. Would you please show me the quarantine certificate and the shipping documents?
请您出示检疫证书和货运单。

7. I'll sterilize the means of transportation and the means of loading and unloading in warehouse. 我要对货物、运输工具及装卸器具进行消毒处理。

8. Sign and issue a quarantine pass notice. 签发"检疫放行通知单"。

9. These objects require to be declared. 这些物品必须申报。

10. These objects must be returned or destroyed. 这些物品必须做退回或销毁处理。

11. These objects require to be quarantined on the spot. 这些物品需要进行现场检疫。

12. I want to inspect food fuselage and passenger fuselage. 我想检查一下食品舱和客舱。

13. Excuse me, who is the owner of these goods? 请问谁是货主?

14. May I see your passport, please? 我可以看你的护照吗?

15. Your passport and declaration card, please. 请出示你的护照和海关申请单。

16. Please have your customs declaration form ready. 请准备好海关申请表。

17. May I have your passport, customs declaration form and health certification forms, please?
请出示护照、海关申请表和健康证明表。

18. Sorry, your passport has expired. 对不起,你的护照已经过期了。

19. You must have a valid visa on your passport. 你的护照必须有有效签证。

Listening 🎧

===== Useful Expressions =====

personal effects 私人物品	pay duty 交税
in the duty-free shop 在免税商店里	in that case 那样的话
declaration form 海关申请表	a trade convention 商务会议
egg tarts 蛋挞	smuggle in by the thousands 成千人的走私

Pair work：Listen to the dialogues and fill in the blanks.

音频 20 - 1

━━━ Dialogue 1 ━━━

Customs（1）

A: Would you please open your _____ , please?

B: All right.

A: These are just _____ effects?

B: That's right. Nothing _____ , I think.

A: Thank you. You may close it now. Anything to _____ ?

B: I have two bottles of _____ with me. I don't know whether I have to _____ duty on them or not.

A: Were they _____ in the duty-free shop?

B: Yes. At the _____ .

A: In that case, you don't have to pay _____ on them.

B: Thank you.

A: You're _____ .

音频 20 - 2

━━━ Dialogue 2 ━━━

Customs（2）

A: May I see your _____ , please?

B: Here is my passport. And this is the _____ form.

A: What is the _____ of your visit to the United States?

B: Business. I have a trade convention I'm _____ in Chicago.

A: This visa is good for two weeks. Do you _____ to stay longer than that?

B: No. I will fly _____ twelve days from now on.

A: And you will do some _____ while you are here?

B: Yes. I want to spend a couple days in New York. I have _____ there I will visit.

A: What do you have in the bag, Mr. Lee?

B: Just my _____ , my clothes，and some books.

A: You're not _____ any food with you today?

B: No.

A: Okay，Mr. Lee. This is just a routine _____ . Would you _____ opening the bag for me?

B: Alright.

A: Hmm. You have three _____. Are you a photographer?

B: No, my _____ makes cameras. Well, I'm also a photographer, but two of these are for our _____.

A: I see. And what's in this _____?

B: Egg tarts.

A: I thought you said you didn't have any _____with you today.

B: I thought you _____ vegetables and meat when you asked me. Things _____ that. I don't have any _____.

A: I'm sorry, Mr. Lee. Egg _____are food too. We will have to _____ these.

B: Confiscate?

A: Yes, we will have to _____of them.

B: It's too bad. They are very _____.

A: I know. One out of every three _____ from Taiwan seems to be carrying them. They are being _____ in by the thousands.

B: Oh, well. Not by me.

A: No, not today at least. _____ your visit to the United States, Mr. Lee.

B: Thank you.

⋯⋯⋯ Part III　Practicing ⋯⋯⋯

Reading

=== New Words and Phrases ===

authority [ɔːˈθɒrəti] n. 权威；权力；学术权威

agency [ˈeɪdʒənsi] n. 代理；机构；力量

tariff [ˈtærɪf] n. 关税；关税表；价格表

hazardous [ˈhæzədəs] adj. 冒险的；有危险的；碰运气的

verify [ˈverɪfaɪ] v. 核实；证明；判定

apprehend [ˌæprɪˈhend] v. 理解；逮捕，拘押

impede [imˈpiːd] v. 阻碍；妨碍；阻止

deem [diːm] v. 认为，视为；主张，断定

enforce [ɪnˈfɔːs] v. 加强；强迫服从；实施，执行

attain [əˈteɪn] v. 达到，获得；遂愿

constitute [ˈkɒnstɪtjuːt] v. 构成，组成；制定，设立；等同于；指派

privatize [ˈpraɪvətaɪz] v. 使私有化；使归私有

applicable [əˈplɪkəbl] adj. 适当的；可应用的

plug [plʌg] n. 插头；塞子；消防栓；火花塞 v. 插上插头；插入；塞住；〈俚〉枪击，殴打

loophole [ˈluːphəʊl] n. 漏洞；枪眼；观察孔

escalate [ˈeskəleɪt] v. 使逐步升级；使逐步上升；乘自动梯上升

159

allege [əˈledʒ] v. 断言，宣称

immigration authorities 移民当局

appropriate documentation 适当的文件

be entitled to 有……的资格

international arrest warrants 国际逮捕令

customs area 海关区

a bonded store 保税仓库

clear customs 通过海关

a legal declaration 法律声明

prosecute for 起诉

a false declaration 虚假声明

a customs union 关税联盟

value-added tax 增值税

excise duties 土产税

be subject to 受支配；从属于；可以……的；常遭受……

in a bid to do 力图

mitigate corruption 减轻腐败

pre-shipment inspection agencies 装运前检验机构

the declared value 申报价值

be obliged to 必须；不得不；只得

assess duties and taxes 评税

at the port of entry 在入境口岸

protect revenue 保障收益

evasion of customs duty 逃避关税

take over 接管；帮……学习；在……上花费

a fatal remedy 致命的救济

🦢 **Work individually**：Read the following passage and then paraphrase.

Customs

Customs is an authority or agency in a country responsible for collecting tariffs and for controlling the flow of goods, including animals, transports, personal effects, and hazardous items, into and out of a country. The movement of people into and out of a country is normally monitored by immigration authorities, under a variety of names and arrangements. The immigration authorities normally check for appropriate documentation, verify that a person is entitled to enter the country, apprehend people wanted by domestic or international arrest warrants, and impede the entry of people deemed dangerous to the country. In many places, K9 units are also used.

Each country has its own laws and regulations for the import and export of goods into and out of a country, which its customs authority enforces. The import or export of some goods may be restricted or forbidden. In most countries, customs is attained through government agreements and international laws. A customs duty is a tariff or tax on the importation (usually) or exportation (unusually) of goods. Commercial goods not yet cleared through customs are held in a customs area, often called a bonded store, until processed. All authorized ports are recognized customs areas.

At airports, customs is the point of no return for all passengers. Once a passenger has cleared customs, they cannot go back.

Red and Green Channels

In many countries, customs procedures for arriving passengers at many international airports and some road crossings are separated into red and green channels. Passengers with goods to declare (carrying goods above the permitted customs limits and/or carrying prohibited items) go through the red channel. Passengers with nothing to declare (carrying goods within the permitted customs limits and not carrying prohibited items) go through the green channel. However, entry into a particular channel constitutes a legal declaration, if a passenger going through the green channel is found to be carrying goods above the customs limits or prohibited items, he or she may be prosecuted for making a false declaration to customs, by virtue of having gone through the green channel. Each channel is a point of no return. Once a passenger has entered a particular channel, they cannot go back.

Australia, Canada, New Zealand and the United States do not officially operate a red and green channel system; however, some airports copy this layout.

Blue Channel

Airports in EU countries such as Finland, Ireland or the United Kingdom, also have a blue channel. As the EU is a customs union, travelers between EU countries do not have to pay customs duties. Value-added tax and excise duties may be applicable if the goods are subsequently sold, but these are collected when the goods are sold, not at the border. Passengers arriving from other EU countries go through the blue channel, where they may still be subject to checks for prohibited or restricted goods. Luggage tickets for checked luggage travelling within the EU are green-edged so they may be identified. In most EU member states, travelers coming from other EU countries can simply use the green lane.

Red Point Phone

All airports in the United Kingdom operate a channel system, however some don't have a red channel, they instead have a red point phone which serves the same purpose.

Privatizations of Customs

Customs is part of one of the three basic functions of a government, namely: administration; maintenance of law, order, and justice; and collection of revenue. However, in a bid to mitigate corruption, many countries have partly privatized their customs. This has occurred by way of contracting preshipment inspection agencies, which examine the cargo and verify the declared value before importation occurs. The country's customs is obliged to accept the agency's report for the purpose of assessing duties and taxes at the port of entry.

While engaging a preshipment inspection agency may appear justified in a country with an inexperienced or inadequate customs establishment, the measure has not been able to plug the loophole and protect revenue. It has been found that evasion of customs duty escalated when preshipment agencies took over. It has also been alleged that involvement of such agencies has caused shipping delays. Privatization of customs has been viewed as a fatal remedy.

Speaking

New Words and Phrases

immigrant ['ɪmɪgrənt] *n.* 移民，侨民

sightseeing ['saɪtsiːɪŋ] *n.* 观光，游览

luggage ['lʌgɪdʒ] *n.* 行李

baggage ['bægɪdʒ] *n.* 行李

investigate [ɪn'vestɪgeɪt] *v.* 调查；研究；审查

get baggage 取得行李

claim tag 行李票

Pair work：Listen to the dialogues and have a role play.

=== Dialogue 1 ===

音频 20 - 3

Entering a Country

A: May I see your passport，please?

B: Here is my passport. / Here it is.

A: What's the purpose of your visit? Immigrant，sightseeing or business?

B: Sightseeing.

A: How much money do you have with you?

B: I have 10,000 dollars.

A: Good. Have a nice day.

B: Thank you.

=== Dialogue 2 ===

音频 20 - 4

Luggage

A: Where can I get my baggage? I can't find my baggage. Here is my claim tag.

B: Could you please check it urgently? How many pieces of baggage have you lost? Can you describe your baggage?

A: It is a large leather suitcase with my name tag. It's dark blue.

B: Please wait for a moment while we are investigating. Would you come with me to the office?

A: Thank you. I would not like to. Please deliver the baggage to my hotel as soon as you find it.

B: OK.

Unit 21 Claim

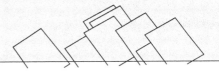

In this unit, the students are required to grasp the following contents.

1. Learning to talk something about claim with some given useful words and phrases of this unit freely.
2. Learning to talk something about claim with some given useful sentences of this unit freely.
3. Reading a passage about claim and then paraphrasing it.
4. Listening and having a role play about claim.

······· Part I Preparing ·······

 Work individually: What contents does claim include?

About claim	Often	Sometimes	Never
A statement from a client in which he holds Maersk liable for a financial loss and requests compensation			
Proper Claims Handling is an essential part of providing good customer service			
Claim by client			
Claim by third party			
Claims Handling Process			
Receipt of claim			
Contract parties			

 Pair work: Compare your answers with a partner.

Do you know anything about claim?

⋯⋯⋯⋯ Part II   Performing ⋯⋯⋯⋯

Reading

════ New Words and Phrases ════

claimee [kleɪm'iː] *n.* 被索赔人

claimant ['kleɪmənt] *n.* 索赔人

claim [kleɪm] *n.* 索赔；赔偿；赔偿金

compensate ['kɒmpenseɪt] *v.* 赔偿，补偿

claimsman ['kleɪmzmən] *n.* 损失赔偿结算人

claims expenses 理赔费用

some different types of claims 索赔的不同类型

a claim on quality 质量索赔

a claim on short weight 短重索赔

a claim on delayed shipment 延期装运索赔

claims assessor 估损人

claims settling agent 理赔代理人

claims surveying agent 理赔检验代理人

claiming administration 索赔局

claims department 索赔委员会

claim letter 索赔书

claims documents 索赔证件

claim report 索赔报告

claims statement 索赔清单

claims settlement 理赔

claims settling fee 理赔代理费

claims rejected 拒赔

insurance claim 保险索赔

settle a claim 解决索赔（问题）

withdraw a claim 撤销（某项）索赔

waive a claim 放弃索赔（要求）

claim on the goods 对某（批）货索赔

claim on sb. 向某人（方）提出索赔

claim for trade dispute 贸易纠纷（引起的）索赔

claim for indemnity 要求索赔

claim for compensation 要求补偿

claim for short weight 由于短重而索赔

claim for damage 由于损坏而索赔

claim for loss and damage of cargo 货物损失索赔

claim for inferior quality 由于质量低劣而索赔

claim against carrier 向承运人索赔

to make a (one's) claim 提出索赔

make a claim for (on) sth. 就某事提出索赔

 Group work：Read the following sentences and learn how to use them freely.

1. Claims occur frequently in international trade. 国际贸易中经常发生索赔现象。

2. We are now lodging a claim with you. 我们现在向贵方提出索赔。

3. I've heard that you have lodged a claim against us. 听说你们已经向我们提出了索赔。

4. We've given your claim our careful consideration. 我们已经就你们提出的索赔做了仔细研究。

5. We lodged a claim with you on fertilizer yesterday.
   昨天我们就化肥问题向贵方提出索赔。

6. We filed a claim with (against) you for the short weight.

关于短重问题，我们已经向你方提出索赔。

7. The Chinese representative and Mr. Bake discussed the claim.

中方代表与贝克先生商谈了索赔问题。

8. We have received the letters giving full details of this claim.

我们已经收到了内容详尽的索赔信件。

9. Sometimes the shipping company or insurance company is found to be responsible for the claim. 有时候，船公司或保险公司应负责赔偿。

10. I was asked to come to your company on my way home in order to settle the claim.

我顺路来你们公司是为了处理索赔问题的。

11. We have received your remittance in settlement of our claim.

我们已经收到你方解决我们索赔问题的汇款。

12. Claims for incorrect material must be made within 60 days after arrival of the goods.

有关不合格材料的索赔问题必须在货到后 60 天内予以解决。

13. I want to settle our claim on you for the 100 tons of bleached cotton waste，as per Sales Confirmation No. 1254E.

我们想处理一下关于销售确认书第 1254E 号 100 吨漂白废棉的索赔问题。

14. We have already made a careful investigation of the case.

我们已经对这个索赔案件做了详细的调查研究。

15. We are not in a position to entertain your claim. 我们不能接受你们提出的索赔要求。

16. But we regret our inability to accommodate your claim.

很抱歉我们不能接受你方索赔。

17. We may consider withdrawing the claim. 我们可以考虑撤回索赔要求。

18. I'll write to our home office to waive our claim immediately.

我立即写信给我们的总公司提出放弃索赔。

19. I'm afraid you should compensate us by 5％ of the total amount of the contract.

恐怕贵公司要赔偿我方合同全部金额的 5％。

20. I propose we compensate you by 3％ of the total value plus inspection fee.

我想我们赔偿贵方 3％ 的损失，另外加上商检费。

21. Claim on short weight is caused by packing damage or short loading.

短重索赔是由包装破损或装运短重引起的。

22. Claim on delayed shipment is that sellers fail to make the delivery according to time schedule.

延期索赔是对卖方没有按时装运货物而提出的索赔。

23. Claim on quality originates from inferior quality of goods or quality changes.

品质（质量）索赔是在货物质量低劣或是质量改变的条件下发生的。

Listening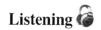

━━━━━━ Useful Expressions ━━━━━━

easy to break and easy to burst 易断易爆裂
the unqualified product 不合格的产品
lost a lot of money 巨大经济损失
seasonal goods 季节货物
necessary documentation 必要文件
insurance company 保险公司
decline claim 拒绝索赔

ISO international standard ISO 国际标准
something unpleasant 不愉快的事
Christmas candles 圣诞蜡烛
contract stipulations 合同规定
the shipping advice 装船通知
actual distribution 实际销售

Pair work： Listen to the dialogues and fill in the blanks.

━━━━━━ Dialogue 1 ━━━━━━

Following ISO International Standard

音频 21 - 1

A: Look，this is your _____! Easy to break and easy to _____!

B: Oh，that's not true. It was _____ because of the improper usage.

A: Improper? Look! This is your _____ and we just _____ what it says. And according to the ISO international _____, this should be classified as the _____ product! We will return this batch and you should _____ our money.

B: Oh，that's not the _____! Our product _____ is always strictly follow the ISO standard and we get the _____. Maybe this one did have _____ but it doesn't _____ that this batch are all unqualified.

A: Please don't forget our _____! You have promised that your _____ was willing to compensate all _____ for the unqualified products.

B: Yes，that's true. We will _____ pay the unqualified ones but not all products we have sent to you. If you have the _____ certification and tests _____ for all the unqualified products，we will _____ for it.

━━━━━━ Dialogue 2 ━━━━━━

Rejecting a Claim

音频 21 - 2

Amy: I have something _____ to talk over with you, Mr. Dell.

Dell: It's nothing _____, I hope.

Amy: Unfortunately it is. We have lost a lot of _____ because of it.

Dell: You mean the _____ of Christmas candles?

Amy: You know，Christmas candles are _____ goods. We signed a contract for 100,000 dozen Christmas _____ last September. The goods should have _____ in London no later than late November，but it was on December 29 that the candles arrived when it was too _____ for us to have them _____.

Dell: We did have the candles _____ according to the contract _____. You might have _____ it from the shipping _____ we sent you.

Amy: I've studied all the _____ documentation，including the shipping advice. That advice told us the vessel would be sailing for London via Hong Kong and Bombay on October 15. Unfortunately when the _____ called at Bombay，the dockers were on _____，which caused almost ten days _____ in its arrival in London.

Dell: You'd had the cargo _____ against S. R. C. C.，hadn't you? In that case，your claim should be referred to the _____ company for compensation.

Amy: What I'd like to remind you of is that it was stipulated in the contract that the goods would be delivered in early October. If the goods had been delivered before October 10，the strike in Bombay would not have _____ the punctual arrival of the goods. Therefore you are _____ for our loss. The actual distribution started on January 10，half a month later than Christmas. The total loss _____ approximately to €3,000.

Dell: I don't think your claim is _____. I'm afraid I can't help but decline your claim.

······ Part III　Practicing ······

Reading

=== New Words and Phrases ===

error ['erə(r)] *n.* 错误，过失

mishap ['mɪshæp] *n.* 灾祸；不幸事故

deliver [dɪ'lɪvə(r)] *v.* 交付；发表；递送

pilferage ['pɪlfərɪdʒ] *n.* 行窃，偷盗；小偷小摸

prerequisite [ˌpriː'rekwəzɪt] *n.* 先决条件，前提，必要条件

become liable to 变得容易

cargo shortage 货物不足

damage to goods 货物受损

delivery of goods 货物发送

breach of contract 违约，违反合同

a rightful claim 正当要求

live up to 不辜负；履行；达到高标准；实行

a financial loss 财务损失

as a consequence of 由于……，因为……

invoice value of the goods 货物的发票价值

in connection with 与……有关，连同

anticipated lost profit 预期利润损失

unload a container 卸下集装箱

Work individually: Read the following passage and then paraphrase.

Claim Introduction

Errors, mishaps and accidents happen and will at times prevent Maersk from delivering the service the client expected. Sometimes, the client is right in claiming against Maersk and we become liable to pay compensation, and sometimes not. Proper claims handling is an essential part of providing good customer service.

What is a Claim?

A claim is a statement from a client in which he holds Maersk liable for a financial loss and requests compensation. The loss has typically arisen due to cargo shortage, pilferage, damage to goods, late delivery/non-delivery of goods or other forms of breach of contract.

Breach of contract is a situation in which one of the parties to a contract does not fulfill his/her responsibilities. This is a pre-requisite for any of the parties to the contract to file a rightful claim. Someone must have failed to live up to his/her responsibilities.

Claimant

The party who files the claim is called the claimant. A claim does not necessarily lead to payment of compensation but the claim initiates the process of evaluating the cause of loss or damage, establish who is liable and determine if compensation is to paid and if so, how much.

It is important to note that compensation can only be sought from someone who is a party to the contract and only if the claimant has actually suffered a financial loss as a consequence of the contract. A financial loss is typically said to include the invoice value of the goods (buying price from supplier/manufacturer/vendor) incl. any freight/insurance paid but not anticipated lost profit.

Claim Types

In connection with delivering services to our clients, Maersk generally risk two types of claims:

1. Claim by client

The most common type is a claim filed by our client, e. g. for loss of or damage to the goods during transit or storage, misdirection (goods are sent to wrong destination) or misdelivery (release of goods to wrong party). Maersk also receives claims for delays (cargo arrives later than planned) but generally, compensation is not awarded for such unless Maersk can be said to have acted carelessly.

2. Claim by a third party

Another, less common, type is a claim by a third party who is not a party to the contract between Maersk and our client but has nevertheless incurred a loss as a consequence of the contract, e. g. a warehouse operator whose property has been damaged while we unloaded a container.

Claims Handling Process

A number of activities take place from the time a client submits a formal claim to the time the case is concluded. The legal and formal processing of a claim lie with specialists but you may be the one to receive the claim or may need to follow the process if the case influences your relationship with the client.

Overall, the following are the steps in claims handling:

1. Receipt of claim

Request client to forward formal claim in writing and initiate the process of collecting the facts of the case. Notify manager and claims specialist.

2. Establish contract parties

Determine if the client is actually claiming the right party. Is the damage/loss likely to have occurred while the cargo was covered by a contract between Maersk and the client? (Done by lawyer/claims specialist).

3. Establish defences

Analyze the facts of the case and establish any reasons why Maersk should not be held liable for the financial loss incurred by the client. (Done by lawyer/claims specialist)

4. Argue case and determine liability

Explain and discuss our views of the case with the client or his representative. Reach an agreement concerning level of liability, if any. This may take place in or outside court. (Done by lawyer/claims specialist)

5. Determine compensation (if any)

Calculate and pay compensation based on the terms and conditions of the contract or the agreement reached with the client or his representative. (Done by lawyer/claims specialist)

6. Recover loss from subcontractor and/or insurance

If possible, claim against subcontractor to recover all or part of our loss. Investigate if our insurance covers any additional losses. Claim should be filed as early as possible.

7. Take corrective action to prevent future incidents

Record claim, investigate its reasons and evaluate the likelihood of reoccurrence. Take actions through quality assurance, better procedures, training and other initiatives.

Speaking

═══ New Words and Phrases ═══

consignment [kən'saɪnmənt] *n.* 装运的货物，
　　托运的货物；托运，运送

lodge a claim with 向……提出索赔

be not up to 低于

stipulated standard 规定的标准

total amount 全部金额

careful consideration 仔细研究

in apparent good condition 外表良好

shipping manager 货运经理

That goes for us too. 我们也是这么希望的。

Pair work：Listen to the dialogues and have a role play.

音频 21 - 3

═══ Dialogue 1 ═══

Claim（1）

A: We are now lodging a claim with you.

B: Why?

A: This consignment is not up to the standard stipulated in the contract. We are now lodging a claim with you. I'm afraid you should compensate us by 5% of the total amount of the contract.

B: We've given your claim our careful consideration.

A: However，the B/L shows that when the shipping company received the goods，they were in apparent good condition. The liability is certainly not on our side.

B: I know.

═══ Dialogue 2 ═══

Claim（2）

音频 21 - 4

A: What about our claim?

B: Our shipping manager is looking into it.

A: When will we hear something from him?

B: On，in just a day or two，I think.

A: Here is the final settlement for our claim.

B: Thanks. We appreciate how fast you worked.

A: We only hope we won't have this kind of problem again.

B: That goes for us too.

Unit 22 International Logistics

======= Objectives =======

In this unit, the students are required to grasp the following contents.

1. Learning to talk something about international logistics with some given useful words and phrases of this unit freely.

2. Learning to talk something about international logistics with some given useful sentences of this unit freely.

3. Reading a passage about international logistics and then paraphrasing it.

4. Listening and having a role play about international logistics.

······ Part I Preparing ······

 Work individually: What contents does international logistics include?

The logistics process consists of the process of integration of several aspects	Often	Sometimes	Never
Material handling			
Warehousing			
Information			
Transportation			
Packaging			
Inventory			
All of the above			

 Pair work: Compare your answers with a partner.

Do you know anything about international logistics?

•••••• Part II   Performing ••••••

Reading

International logistics terms

A/N	Arrival Notice	到货通知
BAF	Bunker Adjustment Factor	燃油附加费（大多数航线都有，但标准不一）
B/L	Bill of Lading	海运提单
B/R	Buying Rate	买价
C&F	Cost and Freight	成本加运费价
CIF	Cost Insurance and Freight	成本运费加保险，俗称"到岸价"
CPT	Carriage Paid To	运费付至（……目的地）
CIP	Carriage and Insurance Paid To	运费、保险费付至目的地
CY	Container Yard	整柜交货，货柜场
CFS	Cargo Freight Station	集装箱货运站
C/D	Customs Declaration	报关单
CNTR NO.	Container Number	柜号
C/O	Certificate of Origin	原产地证证明书
CTN/CTNS	Carton/Cartons	纸箱
C. S. C	Container Service Charge	货柜服务费
CNEE	Consignee	收货人
CAF	Currency Adjustment Factor	货币汇率附加费
CFS	Container Freight Station	散货仓库，散装交货
CHB	Customs House Broker	报关行
CTNR	Container	货柜
DAF	Delivered at Frontier	边境交货
DES	Delivered Ex Ship	目的港船上交货
DEQ	Delivered Ex Quay	目的港码头交货
DDU	Delivered Duty Unpaid	未完税交货

（续）

DDP	Delivered Duty Paid	完税后交货
DDC	Destination Delivery Charge	目的港码头费
DL/DLS	dollar/dollars	美元
D/P	Document Against Payment	付款交单
DOC	document	文件，单据
DOC	Document Charge	文件费
D/O	Delivery Order	到港通知
ETA	Estimated Time of Arrival	到港日
ETD	Estimated Time of Delivery	开船日
ETC	Estimated Time of Closing	截关日
EBS	Emergency Bunker Surcharges	部分航线燃油附加费的表示方式
EXP	export	出口
EPS	Equipment Position Surcharges	设备位置附加费
Ex	Ex Work/Ex Factory	工厂交货
FOB	Free On Board	离岸价
FCL	Full Container Cargo Load	整箱货
FAF	Fuel Adjustment Factor	燃油价调整附加费
F/F	Freight Forwarder	货运代理
FAK	Free Alongside Ship	装运港船边交货
FIO	Free in and out	指船公司不付装船和卸船费用
FIOST	Free in and out and Stowed and Trimmed	指船公司不负责装、卸、平舱、理舱
FI	Free In	指船公司不付装
FO	Free Out	指船公司不付卸
GRI	General Rate Increase	综合费率上涨附加费（一般是南美航线、美国航线使用）
G. W.	Gross Weight	毛重
G. S. P.	Generalized System of Preferences	普惠制
HB/L	House Bill of Lading	货代提单
HBL	House B/L	子提单
H/C	Handling Charge	代理费
IAC/DDC	Intermodal Administration Charge/ Destination Delivery Charge	美加航线使用，直航附加费

（续）

IFA	Interim Fuel Adjustment	临时燃油附加费（某些航线临时使用）
INV	invoice	发票
IMP	import	进口
INT	international	国际的
LCL	Less Than One Container Cargo Load	拼箱货
L/C	Letter of Credit	信用证
MB/L	Master Bill of Loading	主提单
MIN	minimum	最小的，最低限度的
M/V	Merchant vessel	商船
M/T	Measurement Ton	尺码吨（即货物收费以尺码计费）
MT	metric ton	公吨
MAX	maximum	最大的，最大限度的
MTD	Multimodal Transport Document	多式联运单据
NOVCC	Non Vessel Operating Common Carrier	无船承运人
N. W.	net weight	净重
N/F	notify	通知人
O/F	Ocean Freight	海运费
OB/L	Ocean Bill of Lading	海运提单
OBL	Ocean (or original) B/L	海运提单
OP	Operation	操作
POD	Port of Destination	目地港
POL	Port of Loading	装运港
PSS	Peak Season Surcharges	旺季附加费（大多数航线在运输旺季时可能临时使用）
F/P	Freight Prepaid	运费预付
PCS	Port Congestion Surcharge	港口拥挤附加费（一般被以色列、印度某些港口及中南美航线使用）
PTF	Panama Transit Fee	巴拿马运河附加费（美国航线、中南美航线使用）
PKG	Package	一包，一捆，一扎，一件等
PCE/PCS	piece/pieces	只、个、支等
P/L	packing list	装箱单、明细表

（续）

PCT	percent	百分比
S/O	Shipping Order	订舱单，装货指示书
SEAL NO.	Seal Number	铅封号
S/M	shipping marks	装船标记
THC	Terminal Handling Charge	码头费（香港）
T/T	Telegram Transit	电汇
T. O. C	Terminal Operations Option	码头操作费
T. R. C	Terminal Receiving Charge	码头收柜费
T/S	Trans-Ship	转船
TVC/TVR	Time Volume Contract/ Rate	定期定量合同
TEU 20'	Twenty-Foot Equivalent Unit 20'	柜型
TTL	Total	总共
T, LTX, TX	telex	电传
VOCC	Vessel Operating Common Carrier	船公司
WT	weight	重量
W/T	Weight Ton	重量吨
W/M	Weight or Measurement Ton	即以重量吨或者尺码吨中从高收费
YAS	Yard Surcharges	码头附加费/日元升值附加费（日本航线专用）

 Group work：Read the following sentences and learn how to use them freely.

1. Modern logistics is one of the most challenging and exciting jobs in the world.
   现代物流是世界上最富挑战性和最激动人心的工作。

2. Logistics is part of a supply chain. 物流是供应链的整体组成部分。

3. Logistics is a unique global "pipeline". 物流是独特的全球信道。

4. Logistics is related to the effective and efficient flow of materials and information.
   物流涉及物料和信息的有效、快速流动。

5. Logistics operation and management include packaging, warehousing, material handling, inventory control, transport, forecasting, strategic planning, customer service, etc.
   物流操作和管理包括包装、仓储、物料搬运、库存控制、运输、预测、战略计划和客户服务等方面。

6. Logistics consists of warehousing, transportation, loading and unloading, carrying, packaging, processing, distribution and logistics information.
   物流由仓储、运输、装卸、搬运、包装、加工、配送和物流信息所组成。

7. Logistics may be divided into supply logistics, production logistics, distribution logistics, returned logistics and waste material logistics.

物流可以分成供应物流、生产物流、销售物流、回收物流和废弃物物流。

8. Logistics is now the last frontier for increasing benefits in industrial production.

物流是当今工业生产增加利润的最后领域。

9. Logistics is unique, and it never stops! 物流是独特的，它从不停止。

10. Logistics performance is happening around the globe, twenty-four hours a day, seven days a week and fifty-two weeks a year.

物流运作一天 24 小时、一周 7 天、一年 52 星期在全球发生。

11. Logistics is concerned with getting products and services where they are needed and when they are desired.

物流涉及在需要的时候和在需要的地方取得产品和服务的活动。

12. Logistics is the process of planning, implementing and controlling the efficient, effective flow and storage of goods, services and related information from the point of origin to the point of consumption for the purpose of conforming to customer requirements.

物流是计划实施和控制商品的快速、高效流动和储存，以及从源头到消费的服务和信息的全过程，以满足客户的需求。

13. Logistics is a hot topic in China. 中国掀起了物流热。

14. The overall goal of logistics is to achieve a targeted level of customer service at the lowest possible total cost.

物流的总目标是以最低的总成本实现客户服务的目标水平。

15. It is important that persons involved in day-to-day logistics work have a basic understanding of logistics.

重要的是，从事日常物流工作的人员应对物流有个基本的了解。

16. Logistics must be managed as a core competency.

物流必须作为一个核心能力来管理。

17. Logistics competency directly depends on a firm's strategic positioning.

物流能力是由一家公司的战略定位直接决定的。

18. Logistics service is a balance of service priority and cost.

物流服务是服务优先与成本间的平衡。

19. There are five basic modes of transportation. They are water transport, rail transport, truck transport, air transport and pipeline transport.

基本运输方式有五种，他们是水陆运输、铁路运输、汽车运输、航空运输和管道运输。

20. Transportation is a vital component in the design and management of logistics systems.

运输是物流系统设计和管理中至关重要的组成部分。

Listening

━━━━ **Useful Expressions** ━━━━

be acquainted with 熟悉

specialized logistic company 专业物流公司

the key point 焦点

have an appointment with 和……约会

general manager 总经理

headquarter and warehouse 总部和仓库

establish regular business relations with 与……建立定期业务关系

the inventory system 库存系统

focus on 关注于

save manpower and resources 节省人力资本

in charge of 主管，负责；照料

show sb. around 带……参观

cooperate with 与……协作，合作

Pair work：Listen to the dialogues and fill in the blanks.

音频 22 - 1

━━━━ Dialogue 1 ━━━━

Logistics（1）

A: Hello，sir. So _____ to see you again.

B: Hello. Is there anything _____ I can do for you?

A: Thank you. I want to be acquainted with the _____ system. Would you please ____
_____ me to it?

B: Oh，it's my pleasure. The inventory plays an _____ role in _____.

A: I quite agree with you on that point.

B: Yes. At the inventory system，ABC classification is quite useful. At _____, most
specialized logistic company _____ this way.

A: Could you tell me the _____?

B: ABC classification can make most strength _____ on the key point. It can save
manpower and _____ .

A: Thank you for telling me so _____ .

B: Welcome.

━━━━ Dialogue 2 ━━━━

Logistics（2）

音频 22 - 2

Mary: Hello!

Eric: Hello! I'm Eric.

Mary: Do you have an _____?

Eric: Yes，I have an appointment with your _____. This is the reason. I'm here to build up the _____ relations with your company.

Mary: I'm the secretary of the _____ company. What can I do for you?

Eric: I'd like to see the person in _____ of warehouse.

Mary: I'm so sorry. General manger of our _____ is not in right now. May be I can __ _____.

Eric: It can't be better. Do you have _____?

Mary: Of course. Let me show you _____. I'd like to show you the headquarter and _____.

Eric: I'm interested in that. I'm willing to _____ with your company.

Mary: That's good news for us. We hope to establish _____ business relations with you.

•••••• Part III   Practicing ••••••

Reading

====== New Words and Phrases ======

implementation [ˌɪmplɪmen'teɪʃn] *n.* 贯彻；成就；

logistics [lə'dʒɪstɪks] *n.* 物流；后勤；逻辑学

furnish ['fɜːnɪʃ] *n.* 陈设，布置；提供

intermeshing ['ɪntɜːmeʃɪŋ] *n.* 交互重叠

logistics arrangements 物流安排

military forces 兵马

without reimbursement 无须偿还

a significant element 一个重要的元素

a temporary or permanent basis 临时或永久的基础

landing craft 登陆艇

commercial property 商业财产

vehicle fleet 车队

a logistics administration department 后勤管理部门

Work individually：Read the following passage and then paraphrase.

Logistics

What is international logistics?

The negotiating, planning, and implementation of supporting logistics arrangements between nations, their forces, and agencies. It includes the furnishing of logistics support (major end items, material, and/or services) to, or receiving logistics support from one or more friendly foreign governments, international organizations, or military forces, with or without reimbursement. It also includes the planning and actions related to the intermeshing of a significant element, activity, or component of the military logistics systems or procedures of the United States with those of one or more foreign governments, international organizations, or military forces on a temporary or permanent basis. It includes planning and actions related to the utilization of U. S. logistics policies, systems, and/or procedures to meet requirements of one or more foreign governments, international organizations, or forces.

What are the roles of logistics?

Logistics, by definition is coordinating complex operations involved in the moving of people, equipment, and supplies. It is very important in our daily lives. During World War II alone, the logistics involved in preparing for "D-Day" at Normandy were "awe-inspiring". Not only was the movement of the troops, landing craft, and materials all in need of coordination, but getting those things to the proper areas before the invasion took massive planning. The world could not properly function without logistics.

What is logistics department?

The logistics department is a section of a company which manages logistics to ensure the business is successful. Some of the key aspects of logistics include controlling stock levels, operating storage facilities and transporting goods. The resources used by the logistics department often include finance (managing budgets), people (managing HR) and computer systems (managing IT). Typical assets include commercial property and vehicle fleets.

What are the roles of logistics administration department?

The roles of a logistics administration department is to coordinate with all departments to ensure smooth running of an organization. The department will handle things like communication, transport, training and much more.

Speaking 🎙

New Words and Phrases

packaging ['pækɪdʒɪŋ] *n.* 包装；打包；包装
材料
warehouse ['weəhaʊs] *n.* 仓库，货栈；批发
商店
transportation [ˌtrænspɔː'teɪʃn] *n.* 运送，运
输；运输系统
commit [kə'mɪt] *v.* 犯罪，做错事；把……

托付给
door-to-door 挨家挨户
have an agreement with 同意
sea transportation 海运
with kindest regard 衷心祝好；最亲切的问
候；谨致问候；谨呈真诚的祝愿

音频 22 - 3

Pair work： Listen to the dialogues and have a role play.

===== Dialogue 1 =====

Logistics（3）

A: Welcome to our company. Sir，Nice to meet you.

B: Me too.

A: My name is Gary. It's very kind of you to visit our company . I'm very happy to introduce it.

B: Thanks a lot.

A: Our business covers packaging，warehousing and shipping any taxes and insurance.

B: Do you ship door-to-door?

A: Certainly. All shipments are door-to-door!

B: Oh，I'm happy to hear that!

A: If you have any other questions，please feel free to contact me anytime.

B: Thanks very much.

A: It's my pleasure.

===== Dialogue 2 =====

Logistics（4）

音频 22 - 4

Customer: I am glad that we have an agreement with your company. At present，I want to know what your earliest delivery date is.

Peter: It usually takes us one month to deliver. And for a special order，it takes a little longer. It's two months. In addition，prompt shipment is very important to us.

Customer: Our company has a large amount of goods that we need to deliver. I think your company can do it best.

Peter: Oh. Which transportation do you want?

Customer: Uh，because we hope that our partner wouldn't miss sales season，the sea transportation is very perfect.

Peter: Do you know when the exact shipping date is?

Customer: I want to know the earliest time，because we need to make sure we have enough the time.

Peter: We will try our best to advance shipment，but we cannot commit ourselves.

Customer: I'm glad to hear that. Thank you.

Peter: With kindest regard.

Unit 23 Insurance

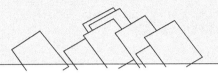

In this unit, the students are required to grasp the following contents.

1. Learning to talk something about insurance with some given useful words and phrases of this unit freely.
2. Learning to talk something about insurance with some given useful sentences of this unit freely.
3. Reading a passage about insurance and then paraphrasing it.
4. Listening and having a role play about insurance.

······· Part I Preparing ·······

 Work individually: What contents does insurance include?

About insurance	Often	Sometimes	Never
Insurance is a means of protection from financial loss			
It is a form of risk management primarily used to hedge against the risk of a contingent, uncertain loss			
An entity which provides insurance			
A person or entity who buys insurance is known as an insured or policyholder			
The insured receives a contract, called the insurance policy			
Premium			

 Pair work: Compare your answers with a partner.

Do you know anything about insurance?

······ **Part II Performing** ······

Reading

=== New Words and Phrases ===

hurricane [ˈhʌrɪkən] n. 飓风

insurability [ɪnʃʊərəˈbɪlɪti] n. 可保性

loading [ˈləʊdɪŋ] n. 附加费

notification [ˌnəʊtɪfɪˈkeɪʃn] n. 告知

priority [praɪˈɒrəti] n. 自负责任

tornado [tɔːˈneɪdəʊ] n. 龙卷风

tariff [ˈtærɪf] n. 费率表

broker [ˈbrəʊkə(r)] n. 经纪人

casualty [ˈkæʒuəlti] n. 意外伤害险

policy [ˈpɒləsi] n. 保单

principal [ˈprɪnsəpl] n. 业主

employer [ɪmˈplɔɪə(r)] n. 业主

reinsurer [riːɪnˈʃʊərər] n. 再保人

reserve [rɪˈzɜːv] n. 准备金

retention [rɪˈtenʃn] n. 自留

professional [prəˈfeʃənl] n. 专业险

catastrophe [kəˈtæstrəfi] n. 巨灾险

sum insured 保额

free from particular average（F. P. A.）平安险

with particular average（W. P. A.）水渍险

excess of loss cover 超额赔偿

all risk 一切险

risk of breakage 破碎险

risk of clashing 碰损险

risk of rust 生锈险

risk of hook damage 钩损险

risk of contamination（tainting）污染险

insurance against total loss only（TLO）全损险

risk of deterioration 变质险

risk of packing breakage 包装破裂险

risk of inherent vice 内在缺陷险

risk of normal loss（natural loss）途耗或自然损耗险

risk of spontaneous combustion 自然险

risk of contingent import duty 进口关税险

insurance against war risk 战争险

insurance against extraneous risks，insurance against additional risks 附加险

risk of theft，pilferage and non-delivery（TPND）盗窃、提货不着险

risk of fresh and/of rain water damage（wetting）淡水雨淋险

risk of leakage 渗漏险

risk of shortage in weight/quantity 短量险

risk of sweating and/or heating 受潮受热险

risk of bad odor（change of flavor）恶味险，变味险

risk of mould 发霉险

on deck risk 舱面险

full coverage 全额承保

full insurance value 足额保险价值

GNPI 总净保费收入

individual losses 单一损失

insurability 可保性

individual losses 单一损失

insured losses 保险损失

light damage 轻度破坏

loss participation 分担损失

loss settlement 损失赔付

moderate damage 中度破坏

susceptibility of goods to water 易受水浸性
terms used in insurance industry accident 意
外事故险

advance loss profits（ALOP）预期利润损失
险，利损险

 Group work：Read the following sentences and learn how to use them freely.

1. In reply to your letter of the 3rd November enquiring about the insurance on our CIF offer for Double offset ring spanners made to you on the 20th October，we wish to give you the following information. 回复你们11月3日询问我们10月20日所报梅花扳手CIF报价有关保险的信函，我们希望给你们下列信息。

2. For transaction concluded on CIF basis... 对CIF基础上成交的交易……

3. We usually effect insurance with The People's Insurance Company of China against all risk，as per Ocean Marine Cargo Clauses of The People's Insurance Company of China. 我们一般按照中国人民保险公司的海洋运输货物保险条款向中国人民保险公司投保一切险。

4. effect insurance against... risk（insure the goods against... risk.）投保……险

5. This transaction is concluded as per your e-mail of 1st March and ours of 3rd March. 这笔交易是按照你方3月1日和我方3月3日的电子邮件达成的。

6. Details as per the attached list. 详见附单。

7. Should you require the insurance to be covered as per institute Cargo Clauses，we would be glad to comply but if there is any difference in premium between the two it will be charged to your account.
假如你们需要按照协会货物保险条款保险，我们也乐于照办，但如果两者保费有所不同，则其差额由你方负担。

8. Should you place orders now we would give you a 5% discount.
假如你现在订货，我们可以给你5%的折扣。

9. Should there be any vessel available this month we would certainly ship the goods.
假如本月有订得到舱位的船，我们肯定装运货物。

10. if there is any difference... ＝should there be any difference
如果有任何不同的话……

11. We are also in a position to insure the shipment against any additional risk if you so desire. 假如希望的话，我们也能对货物投保任何附加险别。

12. The extra premium is to be borne by you. 额外保险费将由你们负担。

13. Your order is to be shipped next month. 你方订单将于下月装运。

14. The detailed specifications are to be sent to you before long. 详细规格不久将寄给你。

15. If a higher percentage is required，we may do accordingly. But you have to bear the extra premium as well.
假如保险金额的百分率要更高些，我们也可以照办，但你们也同样需负担其额外保费。

16. We have remitted you the commission and the rebate as well. 我已经汇付给你佣金和回扣。

17. We hope our above information will provide you with all the information you wish to know. 我们希望上述信息将提供给你们希望了解的一切内容。

18. We would like to inform you that most of our clients are placing their orders with us on CIF basis. 我们希望告诉你方，我们多数客户都按 CIF 向我们订货。

19. Our insurance company is a state operated enterprise enjoying high prestige in settling claims promptly and equitably and has agents in all main ports and regions of the world. 我们的保险公司是国营企业，享有理赔迅速、处理公平的声誉，并在全球各主要港口和地区都有代理。

20. Should any damage occur to the goods，you may file your claim with their agent at your end，who will take up the matter without delay.
假如货物发生损坏，你们可以向他们在你处的代理提出索赔，他们将迅速地办理。

Listening 🎧

━━━━━ **Useful Expressions** ━━━━━

People's Insurance Company of China 中国人民保险公司

the unfortunate affair about the insurance 不幸事件的保险

as far as 只要；远到……；据……；直到……为止

beyond the scope of coverage 超出承保范围

within the scope of coverage 在承保险别范围内

make out 理解；假装；辨认出

an insurance certificate covering W. P. A. 投保水渍险的保险凭证

the risk of breakage 破碎险　　　　　　ring up 给……打电话

the Ceramics Section of Light Industrial Products Import & Export Corporation 轻工业品公司陶瓷品部

in case of breakage 万一破损

 Pair work：Listen to the dialogues and fill in the blanks.

音频 23 - 1

━━━━ Dialogue 1 ━━━━

Insurance（1）

A: Good afternoon，Mr. Brown. My _____ was at 4 o'clock，wasn't it?

B: Yes，Mrs. Wang. We have been _____ you. Mrs. Wang，this is Mr. Jordan of the People's _____ Company of China. He has come to _____ the unfortunate affair about the insurance.

A: Thank you for _____. Mr. Brown, as you may _____, the February consignment arrived at Manila seriously _____. The loss through _____ was over 30% of the _____. We've presented a claim to the _____ through your firm, but the insurance company _____ to admit liability, as there was no insurance on breakage. We naturally were not _____ with such a reply.

B: I should like to _____ what Mr. Jordan has to say about it. You know of course that we, the _____ are merely acting as mediators in this _____. The Insurance Company is _____ for the claim, as far as it is within the _____ of coverage.

J: That's just the _____. The loss in question was _____ the coverage granted by us. According to your _____, we made out an insurance _____ covering W. P. A. and the risk of breakage wasn't _____ in it. We rang up the Ceramics Section of Light _____ Products Import & Export Corporation, but were told that their _____ had not asked for _____ in case of breakage.

═══════ Dialogue 2 ═══════

Insurance（2）

音频 23 - 2

A: Good morning, Mr. /Ms ××. Can we sign the _____ today?

B: Good morning, I am sorry. As some points _____ the contract have not yet been settled, negotiation has to be _____ before the contract is signed.

A: Sure, so, what's the _____?

B: Firstly, it's about the packing. You know the package of _____ should be careful. My suggestion is to use _____ cases.

A: A wooden case is much heavier than a _____. The freight would be _____.

B: It doesn't matter how much the _____ will be. It's Ok.

A: OK, I'll take this _____.

B: Great, thanks. And the second thing is the _____. Well, what's the _____ of payment you usually _____?

A: Irrevocable L/C, the normal payment _____ in international trade.

B: Sure, that'll be fine. And I'd like to have the insurance of the goods _____ at 110% of the total _____ value. Is that all right?

A: No problem. So, do you _____ any problems?

B: No, I think this first _____ will promote future _____ of the trade between us.

A: I hope so. Shall we _____ the contract tomorrow afternoon?

B: Okay. See you then.

A: See you.

▪▪▪▪▪▪ Part III   Practicing ▪▪▪▪▪▪

Reading

▬▬▬ New Words and Phrases ▬▬▬

contingent [kən'tɪndʒənt] *adj.* 依情况而定 的；取决于……的

entity ['entəti] *n.* 实体；实际存在物；本质

policyholder ['pɒləsɪhəʊldə(r)] *n.* 投保人； 保险客户

assuming [ə'sjuːmɪŋ] *conj.* 如果 *v.* 假定； 取得

guaranteed ['ɡærən'tiːd] *adj.* 有保证的；有 人担保的

premium ['priːmɪəm] *n.* 保险费；额外费用； 附加费

sophisticated [sə'fɪstɪkeɪtɪd] *adj.* 复杂的； 精致的；富有经验的；深奥微妙的

constitute ['kɒnstɪtjuːt] *v.* 构成，组成；制 定，设立

trigger ['trɪɡə(r)] *n.* 扳机

fortuitous [fɔː'tjuːɪtəs] *adj.* 偶然发生的，偶 然的

catastrophically [ˌkætə'strɒfɪklɪ] 灾难性地； 灾难地

risk management 风险管理

financial loss 经济损失

hedge against 防止

uncertain loss 不确定的损失

insurance carrier 保险公司

insurance transaction 保险交易

in the form of 用……的形式

in exchange for 交换

in the event of 万一，倘若

a covered loss 承保损失

be reducible to 被还原成

financial terms 财政条款；财政条件；融资 条件

an insurable interest 可保利益

preexisting relationship 先存关系

insurance policy 保单；保险单

set forth 出发；起程；详尽地解释；展示

a claims adjuster 理赔

in Enlightenment era Europe 在启蒙时代的欧洲

Perpetual Assurance Office 永久保证办公室

predicted losses 预测的损失

be similar to 与……相似；类乎

the actual losses 实际损失

a known time 已知时间

a known place 已知地点

a known cause 已知原因

trigger of a claim 引发索赔

beneficiary of the insurance 保险受益人

insurance premium 保险费

adjust losses 调整损失

the probability of loss 损失的概率

the attendant cost 随之而来的成本

 Work individually: Read the following passage and then paraphrase.

Insurance

Insurance is a means of protection from financial loss. It is a form of risk management primarily used to hedge against the risk of a contingent, uncertain loss.

An entity which provides insurance is known as an insurer, insurance company, or insurance carrier. A person or entity who buys insurance is known as an insured or policyholder. The insurance transaction involves the insured assuming a guaranteed and known relatively small loss in the form of payment to the insurer in exchange for the insurer's promise to compensate the insured in the event of a covered loss. The loss may or may not be financial, but it must be reducible to financial terms, and must involve something in which the insured has an insurable interest established by ownership, possession, or preexisting relationship.

The insured receives a contract, called the insurance policy, which details the conditions and circumstances under which the insured will be financially compensated. The amount of money charged by the insurer to the insured for the coverage set forth in the insurance policy is called the premium. If the insured experiences a loss which is potentially covered by the insurance policy, the insured submits a claim to the insurer for processing by a claims adjuster.

Insurance became far more sophisticated in Enlightenment era Europe, and specialized varieties developed.

The first life insurance policies were taken out in the early 18th century. The first company to offer life insurance was the Amicable Society for a Perpetual Assurance Office, founded in London in 1706 by William Talbot and Sir Thomas Allen. Edward Rowe Mores established the Society for Equitable Assurances on Lives and Survivorship in 1762.

Insurability

Risk which can be insured by private companies typically shares seven common characteristics:

1. **Large number of similar exposure units.** Since insurance operates through pooling resources, the majority of insurance policies are provided for individual members of large classes, allowing insurers to benefit from the law of large numbers in which predicted losses are similar to the actual losses.

2. **Definite loss.** The loss takes place at a known time, in a known place, and from a known cause.

3. **Accidental loss.** The event that constitutes the trigger of a claim should be fortuitous, or at least outside the control of the beneficiary of the insurance.

4. **Large loss.** The size of the loss must be meaningful from the perspective of the insured. Insurance premiums need to cover both the expected cost of losses, plus the cost of issuing and administering the policy, adjusting losses, and supplying the capital needed to reasonably assure that the insurer will be able to pay claims. For small losses, these latter costs may be several times the size of the expected cost of losses. There is hardly any point in paying such costs unless the protection offered has real value to a buyer.

5. **Affordable premium.** If the likelihood of an insured event is so high, or the cost of the event so large, that the resulting premium is large relative to the amount of protection offered, then it is not likely that the insurance will be purchased, even if on offer.

6. **Calculable loss.** There are two elements that must be at least estimable, if not formally calculable: the probability of loss, and the attendant cost.

7. **Limited risk of catastrophically large losses.** Insurable losses are ideally independent and non-catastrophic, meaning that the losses do not happen all at once and individual losses are not severe enough to bankrupt the insurer; insurers may prefer to limit their exposure to a loss from a single event to some small portion of their capital base.

Speaking

New Words and Phrases

validity [vəˈlɪdəti] *n.* 效力；正确性；有效，合法性

expire [ɪkˈspaɪə(r)] *v.* 期满；文件、协议等（因到期而）失效

presume [prɪˈzjuːm] *v.* 推测；以为，认为；假定

explosion [ɪkˈspləʊʒn] *n.* 爆发；爆炸，炸裂

collision [kəˈlɪʒn] *n.* 碰撞；冲突

letter of credit 信用证

various risks clauses 各种风险条款

insurance certificates 保险证书

marine risks 海险

import license 进口许可证

run up to 达到，积累到

natural calamities 自然灾害

maritime accidents 意外事故

carrying vessel 装货船只

be attributable to 可归因于

outside the scope of the coverage 超出保险范围

insurance coverage 保险责任范围

in complying with 遵守

additional cost 额外成本

normal coverage 正常范围

at regular rates 定期利率

insurance agent 保险公司，保险代理人

 Pair work: Listen to the dialogues and have a role play.

音频 23 - 3

 Dialogue 1

Insurance（3）

B: In the letter of credit only coverage for all marine risks was requested. I should like to point out that our prices were calculated without insurance for any special risk. So we applied for the usual W. P. A. coverage and let our customers deal with the matter of breakage. Since the validity of the letter of credit was going to expire in two days, there was no time to write for more detailed instructions. If the L/C had been valid for a longer period, we should have had time to make the matter thoroughly clear.

A: Mr. Brown, our import license only ran up to the middle of February, consequently we were not able to extend the validity of the letter of credit. But we presume that the wording of our L/C implies covering the risk of breakage. Besides, when I take a W. P. A. insurance, that is, with particular average, I should think the risk of breakage is a particular average, isn't it?

J: Not every breakage is a particular average. It is a particular average when the breakage results from natural calamities or maritime accidents, such as stranding and sinking of the carrying vessel, or is attributable to fire, explosion or collision. If none of these conditions occur, breakage is often considered as an ordinary loss and represents what we call inherent vice or nature of the subject matter insured which is outside the scope of the coverage.

Dialogue 2

Insurance（4）

音频 23 - 4

Helen: I'm calling to discuss the level of insurance coverage you've requested for your order.

Henry: I believe that we have requested an amount of twenty-five percent above the invoice value.

Helen: Yes, that's right. We have no problem in complying with your request, but we think that the amount is a bit excessive.

Henry: We've had a lot of trouble in the past with damaged goods.

Helen: I can understand your concern. However, the normal coverage for goods of this type is to insure them for the total invoice amount plus ten percent.

Henry: We would feel more comfortable with the additional protection.

Helen: Unfortunately, if you want to increase the coverage, we will have to charge you extra for the additional cost.

Henry: But the insurance was supposed to be included in the quotation.

Helen: Yes, but we quoted you normal coverage at regular rates.

Henry: I see.

Helen: We can, however, arrange the extra coverage. But I suggest you contact your insurance agent there and compare rates.

Henry: You're right. It might be cheaper on this end.

Helen: Fax me whatever rates you find there and I'll compare them with what we can offer.

参考文献

〔1〕http://www.xuexila.com/yingyu/shangwu/483371.html

〔2〕https://wenku.baidu.com/view/c36

〔3〕http://bbs.fobshanghai.com/thread-1753910-1-1.html

〔4〕http://www.tingroom.com/listen/essay/99811.html

〔5〕http://www.enguo.com/hy/? tid＝363570

〔6〕http://bbs.spiiker.com/topic-11464.html

〔7〕http://blog.sina.com.cn/s/blog_551459dd01012ns8.html

〔8〕http://kaoshi.china.com/bec/learning/601249-1.htm

〔9〕http://www.tingvoa.com/html/20100329/16580.html

〔10〕http://www.tingvoa.com/html/20100329/16580.html

〔11〕http://www.gkstk.com/article/wk-6002890833899.html

〔12〕http://www.tingvoa.com/html/20091129/9498.html

〔13〕http://www.51test.net/show/69167.html

〔14〕https://wenku.baidu.com/view/c01357d380eb6294dd886c04.html

〔15〕http://www.hxen.com/word/changyong/2008-12-23/64095.html

〔16〕https://wenku.baidu.com/view/05481ad780eb6294dd886c5b.html

〔17〕https://wenku.baidu.com/view/05a0106fa45177232f60a294.html

〔18〕https://wenku.baidu.com/view/c6e82e5fdd3383c4ba4cd279.html? re＝view

〔19〕https://wenku.baidu.com/view/a4bf9dd528ea81c758f5783e.html

〔20〕https://wenku.baidu.com/view/769edc36bd64783e09122b5e.html

〔21〕https://wenku.baidu.com/view/36d9aba3b0717fd5360cdc2f.html? re＝view

〔22〕https://wenku.baidu.com/view/d15c36e1bb68a98270fefa89.html

〔23〕https://wenku.baidu.com/view/e1863731650e52ea551898f3.html

〔24〕https://wenku.baidu.com/view/4b0f7673f242336c1eb95e22.html

〔25〕https://wenku.baidu.com/view/290f7ae8f8c75fbfc77db21c.html? re＝view

〔26〕https://wenku.baidu.com/view/d37f9a19fad6195f312ba68a.html

〔27〕https://wenku.baidu.com/view/99028bd6240c844769eaee68.html

〔28〕https://wenku.baidu.com/view/17d3687102768e9951e738e5.html? re＝view

〔29〕https://wenku.baidu.com/view/9b4235490b4e767f5acfce6b.html

〔30〕https://wenku.baidu.com/view/8d27dc35af45b307e8719761.html? re＝view

〔31〕https://wenku.baidu.com/view/9b4235490b4e767f5acfce6b.html? re＝view

〔32〕https://wenku.baidu.com/view/8d27dc35af45b307e8719761.html? re＝view

〔33〕https://wenku.baidu.com/view/cde8b304e87101f69e3195b5.html? re＝view

〔34〕https://wenku.baidu.com/view/2d1d7a51ad02de80d4d8405d.html? re＝view

〔35〕https://wenku.baidu.com/view/4c364c346137ee06eef9182e.html

［36］https://wenku. baidu. com/view/4c364c346137ee06eef9182e. html

［37］https://wenku. baidu. com/view/43e819956f1aff00bfd51e4d. html

［38］https://wenku. baidu. com/view/e1863731650e52ea551898f3. html

［39］http://www. en8848. com. cn/BEC/waimao/wmjxdh/170232. html

［40］https://wenku. baidu. com/view/43e819956f1aff00bfd51e4d. html

［41］https://zhidao. baidu. com/question/159776641. html

［42］http://www. kekenet. com/kouyu/201206/186972 _ 2. shtml

［43］http://www. en8848. com. cn/BEC/kouyu/smdh/186826. html

［44］https://en. wikipedia. org/wiki/Customs

［45］"customs". Word Reference. Retrieved 2013-09-16.

［46］Chowdhury, F. L. (1992) Evasion of Customs Duty in Bangladesh, unpublished MBA dissertation submitted to Monash University, Australia.

［47］"Dual-Channel System (Customs Clearance)". Retrieved 2015-09-02.

［48］Archived March 19, 2009, at the Wayback Machine.

［49］Ec. europa. eu. 2007-02-21. Retrieved 2012-01-06.

［50］http://ec. europa. eu/taxation _ customs/resources/images/etiquette _ verte. gif

［51］Chowdhury, F. L. (2006) Corrupt bureaucracy and privatization of Customs in Bangladesh, Pathok Samabesh, Dhaka.

［52］European Commission-Taxation and Customs Union: The single administrative document (SAD)

［53］"Federation of International Trade Associations, country profile : United States". Fita. org. Retrieved 2012-01-06.

［54］高增安. 商务英语：实用英语丛书［M］. 合肥：中国科学技术大学出版社，2006.

［55］阮绩智，张彦. 商务英语［M］. 杭州：浙江大学出版社，2011.

［56］白善烨. 超级商务英语口语［M］. 洪寅善，译. 长春：吉林摄影出版社，2014.

［57］李雪. 商务英语口语大全［M］. 北京：机械工业出版社，2015.

［58］卡宁海姆. 商务英语［M］. 王珍瑛，李剑宜，译. 青岛：青岛出版社，2017.

［59］吴翠华. 商务英语［M］. 武汉：武汉理工大学出版社，2013.

［60］王峥. 商务英语［M］. 北京：电子工业出版社，2013.

［61］杜清萍. 商务英语［M］. 北京：中国质检出版社（原中国计量出版社），2009.

［62］周邦友. 商务英语［M］. 上海：东华大学出版社，2011.

［63］余慕鸿，章汝雯. 商务英语谈判［M］. 北京：外语教学与研究出版社，2005.